The
Impostor
Sister Lucy

Mike Mains

Contents

A Note to the Reader

Before going any further, look again at the photographs on the front and back cover of this book. Do they look like the same woman to you? If you believe they are, then this isn't the right book for you. Put it aside and pick up another. Reading this book will only send you into a tailspin of mouth-stuttering, spittle-flying cognitive dissonance. You might even faint.

On the other hand, if you can spot the obvious difference between the two women in the photos, then by all means, keep reading. The story presented here just might save your soul.

The information contained in this book was compiled from different sources, chief among them are the books *Our Lady of Fatima* by William Thomas Walsh, and *The Truth about What Really Happened to the Catholic Church after Vatican II* by Brother Michael Dimond and Brother Peter Dimond, along with the websites www.MostHolyFamilyMonastery.com, www.VaticanCatholic.com, and www.SisterLucyTruth.org.

I strongly urge you to read both books and to visit the three websites mentioned above. Brothers Michael and Peter Dimond were the first ones anywhere in the world to pose the question of an impostor Sister Lucy. They are at the forefront of educating us all about the end times we are currently living in and the state of apostasy that exists today in Rome. Don't take my word for it. Read their material and judge for yourself. Your salvation depends on it.

www.SisterLucyTruth.org is an evidence-based website run by Dr. Peter Chojnowski that contains a wealth of information pointing to an impostor Sister Lucy, including facial recognition reports, plastic surgery reports, dental reports, handwriting analysis, comparison photos, you name it. It's impossible to visit this website and not come away with an informed opinion about the question of an impostor Sister Lucy. Once again, don't take my word for it. Visit the site and judge for yourself.

Chapter 1

A Brief History of Fatima

Our Lady of Fatima by William Thomas Walsh is a beautiful book, highly recommended, and if you haven't already read it, then you absolutely must put it first on your reading list after finishing this book. It describes the events that occurred at Fatima in breathtaking fashion.

In 1910, a revolution took place in Portugal and a new republic was formed, led by a collection of Freemasons (Satanists), Marxists, and atheists who all burned with an intense hatred of Jesus Christ and the Catholic Church. Between 1910 and 1916, thousands of Portuguese priests, monks and nuns were brutally murdered, their entrails and decapitated heads paraded through the streets to frighten the populace.

Many more priests and nuns were forced to flee the country. Churches were closed and burned, Church property was confiscated, and the faithful were persecuted. That is the backdrop in which the events of Fatima unfolded.

1

In the summer of 1916, Lucy Santos, age 9, and her two young cousins, Francisco Marto, soon to be 8-years-old, and Jacinta Marto, age 6, were tending their sheep on the hilly slopes of Fatima, Portugal, when they received a vision of a "transparent young man," aged 14 or 15-years-old.

"Don't be afraid," he told the children. "I am the Angel of Peace. Pray with me." The angel kneeled on the ground and said, "My God, I believe, I adore, I hope, and I love you. I beg pardon of You for those who do not believe, do not adore, do not hope, and do not love You."

The angel spoke this prayer three times and the children repeated it. "Pray thus," the Angel said. "The hearts of Jesus and Mary are attentive to the voice of your supplications." Following these words, the Angel dissolved in the sunlight.

Several weeks later, the children received another visit from the Angel. He said to them, "What are you doing? Pray. Pray a great deal. The hearts of Jesus and Mary have merciful designs for you. Offer prayers and sacrifices constantly to the Most High."

The Angel then told the children he was the Guardian Angel of Portugal and disappeared.

Months later, the children received a third and final visit from the Angel. He appeared before them holding a Host and Chalice. The Angel left the Host and Chalice suspended in the air, knelt down, and prayed, "Most Holy Trinity, Father, Son, Holy Ghost, I adore you profoundly and offer You the most precious Body, Blood, Soul and Divinity of Jesus Christ, present in all the tabernacles of the earth, in reparation for the outrages, sacrileges, and indifference with which He Himself is offended. And through the infinite merits of His Most Sacred Heart and of the Immaculate Heart of Mary, I beg of You the conversion of poor sinners."

The Angel offered Communion to Lucy and the Chalice to Francisco and Jacinta, and then disappeared. Afterwards, Francisco said, "I felt that God was in me."

On Sunday, May 13, 1917, the children, now aged ten, nine and seven, were tending their sheep when they saw a flash of lightning, followed by a ball of light, and in the center of the light stood, in Lucy's words, "a lady, all of white, more brilliant than the sun."

The beautiful lady of light appeared to be fifteen or sixteen-years-old. She told the children she was from Heaven and asked them to return to the same spot at the same time on the thirteenth day for the next five months. Lucy asked if she would one day go to Heaven. The young lady replied in the affirmative.

"And Jacinta?" Lucy asked.

"Also."

"And Francisco?"

"Also, but he will have to say many Rosaries."

(Note: Here we see the utter necessity of praying the Rosary for anyone who hopes to go to Heaven. Pray the Rosary devoutly and you have a chance. Don't pray the Rosary and you likely won't make it.)

Lucy asked the young lady about a pair of local girls who had recently died. The lady replied that one of the girls was now in Heaven, but the other would remain in Purgatory until the end of time.

The young lady asked the children if they were willing to offer themselves to God and to endure suffering as acts of reparation for the sins of the world and for the conversion of sinners. Lucy replied that they would and the lady said, "Then you will have much to suffer. But the grace of God will be your comfort."

The young lady raised the palms of her hands and enveloped the children with streams of light. She said, "Say the Rosary every day to obtain peace for the world and to end the war." Then the children watched her rise into the air and disappear into Heaven.

On June 13, 1917, the children received a second visit from the young lady of light. She told them again to say the Rosary every day. Lucy asked the lady to take her and her two cousins to Heaven. The lady replied, "Yes, Jacinta and Francisco I will take soon. But you remain here for some time more. Jesus wishes to make use of you to have me acknowledged and loved. He wishes to establish in the world the devotion to my Immaculate Heart." She raised her hands and enveloped the children with streams of light.

On July 13, 1917, the young lady appeared to the children for the third time. She said to them, "Continue to say five decades of the Rosary every day in honor of Our Lady of the

Rosary to obtain the peace of the world and the end of the war.... Sacrifice yourself for sinners and say many times, especially when you make some sacrifices: 'Oh, Jesus, it is for your love, for the conversion of sinners and in reparation for sins committed against the Immaculate Heart of Mary.' "

At this apparition, the young lady gave the children three secrets. The First Secret was a vision of hell, described in horrifying detail by Sister Lucy in her memoirs:

> "Our Lady showed us a great sea of fire which seemed to be under the earth. Plunged in this fire were demons and souls in human form, like transparent burning embers, all blackened or burnished bronze, floating about in the conflagration, now raised into the air by the flames that issued from within themselves together with great clouds of smoke, now falling back on every side like sparks in a huge fire, without weight or equilibrium, and amid shrieks and groans of pain and despair, which horrified us and made us tremble with fear. The demons could be distinguished by their terrifying and repellent likeness to frightful and unknown animals, all black and transparent. This vision lasted but an instant. How can we ever be grateful enough to our kind heavenly Mother, who had already prepared us by promising, in the first Apparition, to take us to Heaven. Otherwise, I think we would have died of fear and terror."

The Second Secret, which Sister Lucy also revealed in her memoirs, references devotion to the Immaculate Heart of Mary, along with a prediction and a warning of another world war. The young lady told the children, "You see hell where the souls of poor sinners go. To save them, God wishes to establish in the world the devotion to my Immaculate Heart. If they do what I will tell you, many souls will be saved and there will be peace. The war is going to end, but if they do not stop offending God, another and worse one will begin in the reign of Pius XI.

"When you shall see a night illuminated by an unknown light, know that this is a great sign that God gives you that He is going to punish the world for its crimes by means of war, of persecution of the Church and of the Holy Father.

"To prevent this, I come to ask the Consecration of Russia to my Immaculate Heart and the Communion of Reparation on the first Saturdays. If they listen to my requests, Russia will be converted and there will be peace. If not she will scatter her errors through the world, provoking wars and persecutions of the Church. The good will be martyrized, the Holy Father will have much to suffer, various nations will be annihilated.

"In the end my Immaculate Heart will triumph. The Holy Father will consecrate Russia to me, and it will be converted and a certain period of peace will be granted to the world.

"In Portugal the dogma of the Faith will always be kept.... Tell this to no one. Francisco, yes, you may tell him.

(Francisco was able to see the lady, but he could not hear her words.) When you say the Rosary, say after each mystery, 'Oh my Jesus, pardon us and deliver us from the fire of hell. Draw all souls to Heaven, especially those in most need."

The Third Secret of Fatima which the lady gave to the children is a bone of contention among Fatima scholars. We will discuss it at length in a separate chapter later in this book.

At the time of this July apparition, crowds of believers numbering in the thousands were attending the visitations, but were unable to see the woman. There were many among them who thought the apparitions were a fraud, including Lucy's own mother, and they ridiculed the children. For this reason, Lucy asked the young lady to perform a miracle to show everyone they were telling the truth. She responded that on October 13, 1917, she would "perform a miracle that everyone will have to believe." She also told the children that on the same date she would tell them who she was.

By August 13, 1917, news of the lady from Heaven had spread throughout the entire country of Portugal and beyond. Thousands of people, both believers and scoffers, showed up for this next scheduled apparition, but the children were not there. The Administrator of their local town had kidnapped them. The Administrator threw the children in jail and threatened to boil them in oil if they did not tell him the secrets revealed to them by the mysterious lady of light. The children refused.

At the apparition sight, a huge crowd had assembled and when they learned the children had been kidnapped, they exploded in anger and threatened to riot. They were silenced by a clap of thunder, and then watched in awe as lights, the color of the rainbow, fell from the sky. Their anger quieted.

The Administrator reluctantly released the children and on Sunday, August 19, 1917, the lady from Heaven appeared to the children again. She told them she would still perform the promised miracle at the appointed time on October 13, but that it would not be as great of a miracle as it would have been if the Administrator had not kidnapped them. She also said, "Pray, pray a great deal, and make sacrifices for sinners, for many souls go to hell because they have no one to sacrifice and pray for them."

On September 13, 1917, over thirty thousand onlookers, the largest crowd yet, assembled at the apparition sight. The main highway was so jammed it was impossible to move.

The young lady from Heaven appeared to the children and told them, "Continue to say the Rosary to bring about the end of the war. In October, Our Lord will come also, and Our Lady of the Sorrows of Carmel, and Saint Joseph with the Child Jesus to bless the world.... In October, I will perform the miracle so all will believe."

The apparition ended and the crowd was treated to a shower of white petals cascading down from the sky that dissolved upon touch. Was this a premonition of the promised October miracle?

The Miracle of the Sun

On October 13, 1917, despite a downpour of rain, over seventy thousand people came to the apparition sight to witness the predicted miracle. The night before, there were threats to bomb the children's homes and Lucy's mother told her, "If the lady does not make the miracle, the crowd will kill us." Indeed, the consensus among many in the crowd was that if the miracle did not occur, the children and their families would not leave the area alive. The situation was tense when the children arrived and when midday passed and nothing happened, the crowd began to grumble and threaten violence. Lucy's mother shouted in a shrill voice, "Watch out, daughter!" Then the children fell to their knees and the lady from Heaven appeared to them.

She told the children she wanted a chapel built there in her honor, and added, "I am the Lady of the Rosary."

What happened next is one of the greatest miracles in the history of the world, certainly the greatest miracle since the Resurrection. The rain stopped, the clouds parted, and the sun began to spin in the sky, throwing out rays of multi-colored lights. The crowd of seventy thousand watched first in awe and then in abject terror as the sun detached itself from the sky, danced across the horizon from side to side, and hurtled towards the earth.

The crowd fell to their knees with shrieks and cries of mercy. Many of them audibly confessed their sins, others screamed, "It's the end of the world!" Atheists shouted, "I believe! I believe! I believe!" The sun fell closer and closer, threatening to crush and annihilate them all, before finally stopping and returning in zigzag fashion back to its place in the sky. The crowd remained on their knees in stunned silence for several seconds and then erupted in tearful, joyous shouts of, "Miracle! Miracle!"

While the crowd witnessed the Miracle of the Sun, the children saw a vision of the Blessed Virgin with Saint Joseph at her side, holding the Infant Jesus. Saint Joseph blessed the crowd three times, as did the Holy Child.

The children also saw a vision of Our Lady of Sorrows, meeting her Son Jesus on His way to Calvary, and a third vision of Our Lady of Mount Carmel, crowned as queen of Heaven, with the Infant Jesus on her knee.

Before going on, I want to point out a couple of observations.

First, although the lady from Heaven waited until October 13 to reveal herself as the Lady of the Rosary (the Virgin Mary), the consensus all along of both the children and their families, and the people of Portugal who heard about the apparitions, was that they were indeed being visited by the Blessed Virgin.

Second, these visits by the Virgin and the Angel of Peace, along with the Miracle of the Sun that was seen by thousands of witnesses, both believers and non-believers alike, are stunning confirmations of the necessity for one to hold the true Catholic Faith in order to go to Heaven.

Think about it. Our Lady's appearance to three Catholic children, her insistence on praying the Rosary (she even said Francisco would have to pray many Rosaries in order to go to Heaven), her pleas for penance and making sacrifices, her confirmation of Purgatory, her prediction of Pius XI years before he became pope, the visions of Our Lady of Sorrows and Our Lady of Mount Carmel, the Angel of Peace offering Communion to Lucy and the Chalice to Francisco and Jacinta ... those are all beliefs exclusive to the Catholic Faith.

There's also the Miracle of the Sun itself, confirmed in the Bible in The Apocalypse 12:1: "And a great sign appeared in Heaven: A woman clothed with the sun ..." It doesn't get any clearer than that.

If you're not a traditional Catholic, then I strongly urge you to become one. Your eternal salvation depends on it.

Now when I say traditional Catholic, I mean someone who upholds the traditional Catholic Faith. That means a complete rejection of the changes that came with Vatican II, including the non-Catholic and invalid New Mass, and a complete rejection of the non-Catholic antipopes that followed Vatican II. If you find that shocking, stay tuned, we'll talk more about it later. For now back to our story.

Though it had rained continuously the entire morning, leaving the crowd of thousands drenched and standing in mud, everyone's clothes were now clean and dry and the mud was gone.

Ti Marto, the father of Francisco and Jacinto, told the authors of the book *Fatima: Pilgrimage to Peace* that on the morning of the miracle, their house was filled with visitors, leaving mud and water in every room, even on the tables and beds, but after the Miracle of the Sun the house was completely dry and clean.

In addition to the crowd at Fatima, the Miracle of the Sun was witnessed by thousands of more people up to sixteen miles away. Within minutes of its occurrence, every chapel in every surrounding village was filled to capacity.

Among the seventy thousand who made the pilgrimage to Fatima, many came as unbelievers, including some who came to commit violence, but the extraordinary miracle they saw with their own eyes changed their lives. Those who came to jeer fell to their knees and begged God's forgiveness. Many converted to the Catholic faith on the spot.

Among the unbelievers was Avelino de Almeida, the editor of the-Masonic and fiercely anti-Catholic newspaper *O Seculo*, who came to ridicule the event. Even he was stunned by what he saw. The headline to his article which appeared in *O Seculo* two days later read: "Astounding Things! How the Midday Sun Danced at Fatima; The Apparitions of the Virgin - What the Sign from Heaven Consisted of - Many Thousands of People Affirm a Miracle Occurred - War and Peace."

On October 29, 1917, the publication *Illustracao Portuguesa*, the weekly supplement to *O Seculo*, printed Almeida's more detailed description of the miracle:

"And when I no longer imagined that I was seeing anything more impressive than that noisy but peaceful multitude animated by the same obsessive idea and moved by the same powerful yearning, what did I see on that occasion in the shrubland of Fatima that was truly extraordinary? I saw the rain cease to fall at the predicted time, I saw the dense mass of clouds break up and the Sun - a disc of opaque silver - appear at full zenith and begin a violent and convulsive dance, which a great number of people imagined to be a serpentine dance, so beautiful and resplendent were the colors successively adorning the solar surface ...

"Miracle as the people shouted; natural phenomenon, as the wise say? I don't profess to know right now, but only to affirm to you what *I saw* ... The rest is with Science and with the Church."

When the editor of a Masonic newspaper dedicated to liberalism and the destruction of Christianity confirms a Catholic miracle, it's very telling. Several days after the Miracle, a raiding party of Masons struck under cover of night and desecrated the sight of the apparitions, chopping down a tree on which the Lady had stood and carrying away the tables and flowers that had been set up as a makeshift shrine. *O Seculo* denounced the attack. Was the Miracle of the Sun melting even their most hardest of hearts?

At the June 13 visit, Our Lady had told the children she would soon take Francisco and Jacinta to Heaven, and on April 4, 1919, Francisco died at home. Among his last words were, "Look, mother, what a pretty light there by the door!"

Jacinta died a year later on February 20, 1920. Both children told Lucy they had received additional visits from the Blessed Virgin. Jacinta said that the Virgin confided in her that the reason why most people are condemned to hell is because they commit sins of the flesh.

Jacinta's body was exhumed twice, once in 1935 and again in 1950. Both times, her body was found incorrupt, with no sign of decay, appearing as if she were merely a child sleeping. A miracle in itself.

Lucy became a nun. She continued to receive messages from the Blessed Virgin and also from Jesus, and she was given permission from Jesus to reveal the first two secrets, but not to reveal the Third Secret.

On June 13, 1929, Sister Lucy received a visit from the Blessed Virgin who told her, "The moment has come in which God asks the Holy Father, in union with all the bishops of the world, to make the consecration of Russia to my Immaculate Heart, promising to save it by this means.

"There are so many souls whom the justice of God condemns for sins committed against me, that I have come to ask reparation: sacrifice yourself for this intention and pray."

In 1935, Sister Lucy wrote the first of four chapters of her memoirs. She wrote the second chapter in 1937, and both chapters were published in 1938. The third and fourth chapters of Sister Lucy's memoirs were written in 1941 and published shortly afterwards.

On the night of January 25, 1938, the skies of Europe were ablaze with a fiery red light, never before seen. Sister Lucy recognized it immediately as the "unknown light" that the Blessed Virgin had warned the children about, a sign from Heaven that God was going to "punish the world for its crimes by means of war, and of persecution of the Church and of the Holy Father." World War II began shortly after.

In 1939, Sister Lucy was struck with serious illness and in danger of death. She obtained permission from the Blessed Mother to write out the Third Secret of Fatima, and she did so, on a single sheet of paper. The paper was sealed in an envelope, marked "Not to be opened until 1960," and passed first to the local bishop and then to the pope.

Sister Lucy's Interview with Father Fuentes

Sister Lucy gave her last public interview on December 26, 1957 with Father Fuentes. He described her as looking sad and emaciated. Sister Lucy spoke in great seriousness to

Father Fuentes about the Third Secret of Fatima. This is what she told him:

"Father, the Most Holy Virgin is very sad because no one has paid any attention to Her message, neither the good nor the bad. The good continue on their way, but without giving any importance to Her message. The bad, not seeing the punishment of God actually falling on them, continue their life of sin without even caring about the message. But believe me, Father, God will chastise the world and this will be in a terrible manner. The punishment from Heaven is imminent.

"Father, how much time is there before 1960 arrives, and what will happen then? It will be very sad for everyone, not one person will rejoice at all if beforehand the world does not pray and do penance. I am not able to give any other details because it is still a secret. According to the will of the most Holy Virgin, only the Holy Father and the Bishop of Fatima are permitted to know the secret, but they have chosen to not know it so that they would not be influenced. This is the third part of the message of Our Lady which will remain secret until 1960.

"Tell them, Father, that the Most Holy Virgin told my cousins Francisco and Jacinta, as well as myself, many times, that many nations will disappear from the face of the earth and that Russia will be the instrument of chastisement chosen by Heaven to punish the whole world if we do not beforehand obtain the conversion of that poor nation.

"Father, the Most Holy Virgin did not tell me that we are in the last times of the world, but She made me understand this for three reasons.

"The first reason is because She told me that the devil is about to engage in a decisive battle with the Holy Virgin, and a decisive battle is a final battle where one side will be victorious and the other side will suffer defeat. Hence from now on we are for God or we are for the devil. There is no middle course.

"The second reason is because She said to my cousins as well as to myself that God is giving two last remedies to the world: the Holy Rosary and the Devotion to the Immaculate Heart of Mary. These being the last two remedies, this signifies that there will be no others.

"The third reason is because as always in the plans of Divine Providence, God, before He is about to chastise the world, exhausts all other remedies. Now, when He sees that the world pays no attention whatsoever, then, as we say in our imperfect manner of speaking, He offers us with a certain trepidation the last means of salvation, His Most Holy Mother. It is with a certain trepidation because if you despise and repulse this ultimate means we will not have any more forgiveness from Heaven because we will have committed a sin which the Gospel calls the sin against the Holy Ghost. This sin consists of openly rejecting, with full knowledge and consent, the salvation which He offers.

"Remember that Jesus Christ is a very good Son and that He does not permit that we offend and despise His Most Holy Mother. We have as testimony many centuries of Church history which demonstrate, by the terrible chastisements which have befallen those who have attacked the honor of His Most Holy Mother, how Our Lord Jesus Christ has always defended the honor of his Mother.

"Regarding the Holy Rosary, look, Father, the Most Holy Virgin, in these last times in which we live, has given a new efficacy to the recitation of the Rosary. So much so, that there is no problem, no matter how difficult it is, whether temporal or, above all, spiritual, in the personal life of each one of us, of our families, of the families of the world, or of the religious communities, or even of the life of peoples and nations, that cannot be solved by the Rosary.

"There is no problem, I tell you, no matter how difficult it is, that we cannot resolve by praying the Holy Rosary. With the Holy Rosary, we will save ourselves, we will sanctify ourselves, we will console Our Lord and obtain the salvation of many souls.

"Finally, the devotion to the Immaculate Heart of Mary, Our Most Holy Mother, consists in considering Her as the seat of mercy, of goodness and of pardon, and as the certain door by which we are to enter Heaven."

Sister Lucy dropped bombshells all over that interview.

We have her stunning admission that we are indeed living in the end times. What's more, that was in 1957 which only makes us closer to the end now.

We are told that each of us must exercise personal responsibility. We must choose one side or the other, either God or the devil. Remaining lukewarm by ignoring the message of Fatima is no longer an option. We must take the message to heart if we have any hope of going to Heaven.

We are told of the harsh penalty for ignoring this last means of salvation that God has given to us through the Blessed Mother; a grievous sin committed by those who choose to remain willfully blind.

Finally, we are reassured of the power of the Rosary to overcome any problem, either temporal or spiritual.

A Miracle of Fatima (One of Many)

Countless miracles have been attributed to Our Lady of Fatima, and one of the most incredible occurred in 1945.

As World War II drew to a close, the Japanese high command made several attempts to surrender, but they were rebuffed by the Truman administration. Instead of accepting Japan's surrender, on August 6, 1945, the United States dropped an atomic bomb on Hiroshima, and then another atomic bomb on Nagasaki on August 9, 1945.

The Hiroshima bomb killed 80,000 people instantly and another 50,000 died later from wounds and radiation. President Harry Truman, a 33rd degree Grand Master Freemason, boasted of the bombings, "Man has learned to produce the power of the sun here on earth."

Among the only survivors of the Hiroshima bombing were four Jesuit priests, Hugo Lassalie, Hubert Schiffer, Wilhelm Klensorge, and Hubert Cieslik. They lived only eight blocks from ground zero where the bomb detonated. They were praying the Rosary at the exact time when the bomb hit and they credited the Rosary and the message of Fatima for their survival. Everyone else within a square mile was instantly killed.

Not only did the four priests survive, they suffered only minor scratches and lived for years afterwards. They were examined over 200 times and no trace of radiation was ever found on any of them. Their building was the only one for miles around that wasn't demolished by the blast.

Isn't it time you became a traditional Catholic and began praying the Rosary?

Chapter 2

Conclusive Evidence of an Impostor Sister Lucy

There are numerous lines of evidence that prove to us that Sister Lucy was replaced by an impostor sometime around the year 1960. The timing is significant as 1960 was the year that the Third Secret of Fatima was to be released to the public. Sister Lucy made several statements stating that by the year 1960 the contents of the Third Secret would be clearer to the public. Over a dozen people familiar with the situation who met with Sister Lucy prior to 1960 confirmed this.

In this book, we will concentrate on three specific lines of evidence that prove to us that Sister Lucy was indeed replaced with an impostor:

1) Photographic evidence (still photographs and video footage, before 1960 and after).

2) Verbal evidence (statements made by or attributed to Sister Lucy, before 1960 and after).

3) Written evidence (books and letters written by or attributed to Sister Lucy, before 1960 and after).

Let's start with the photographic evidence as it's the most conclusive, the most overwhelming, and the easiest for most people to follow.

Photographic Evidence

The question of whether or not Sister Lucy was replaced by an impostor can actually be answered in less than three seconds. All one has to do is look at the comparison photographs. Anyone who isn't visually impaired or suffering from cognitive dissonance can easily tell that they are not the same woman.

Take another look at the photos on the front and back cover of this book. The real Sister Lucy is on the left and the woman pretending to be Sister Lucy is on the right. You can clearly see that they are two very different people. The eyes, eyebrows, nose, forehead, chin, teeth, and skin color, as well as the entire facial structure are different.

The real Sister Lucy has an oval-shaped face; the impostor Sister Lucy has a round face.

The real Sister Lucy has dimples on her chin and cheeks; the impostor Sister Lucy has no dimples.

The real Sister Lucy has an olive-colored complexion; the impostor Sister Lucy has pale white skin.

The real Sister Lucy has large, protruding teeth that are somewhat mangled; the impostor Sister Lucy has tiny teeth, very straight and perfectly aligned.

When the real Sister Lucy smiles, the corners of her mouth curl up; when the impostor Sister Lucy smiles, the corners of her mouth curl down.

At www.SisterLucyTruth.org you can find profile photographs of both the real and the impostor Sister Lucy that show huge differences in the shape of the nose and chin.

It's quite obvious to anyone with eyes to see that these are not the same woman.

Recall the words of Father Fuentes who conducted the last public interview of Sister Lucy in 1957. He described her as looking sad and emaciated. The definition of emaciated is "abnormally thin and weak." Today we might call such a person anorexic or looking like skin and bones. We've all seen such people.

Yet in every photograph taken after 1960 that the Vatican claims is Sister Lucy, she looks the exact opposite of how Father Fuentes described her.

Rather than sad and emaciated, this new Sister Lucy is fat and jovial. There's a picture of the impostor Sister Lucy taken in 1963 that appears on the cover of one of the versions of Sister Lucy's published memoirs *Fatima in Lucia's Own Words* in which she's smiling and looks like she weighs 300 pounds. So much for sad and emaciated.

And did I mention the ages of the two women?

In the photographs on the front cover of this book, the picture of the real Sister Lucy on the left was taken in 1944 when she was 37-years-old. The picture of the impostor Sister Lucy on the right side was taken 23 years later in 1967. That would make her 60-years-old. Does she look 60-years-old to you?

There are actresses all over Hollywood, many of whom have had cosmetic surgery in an attempt to look younger, who don't look as young at 60 as the woman claiming to be Sister Lucy does.

Yet we're supposed to believe this is Sister Lucy, now aged 60, even though she appears younger than when she was 37.

On the back cover of this book are more photographs showing the real Sister Lucy on the left and the impostor Sister Lucy on the right. In these pictures, the real Sister Lucy is 37 and the impostor Sister Lucy is much older.

Look at their smiles and especially their teeth.

I asked several dentists if it was possible for the woman with the large protruding teeth in the photograph on the left to cosmetically change her teeth or to have dentures made to look like the tiny straight white teeth of the woman on the right.

Not one of them told me it was possible.

Not one.

Once again, it's clear that these pictures do not portray the same woman. They aren't even close.

In fact, the impostor Sister Lucy in the photo on the back cover of this book might be a different woman than the impostor Sister Lucy in the photo on the front cover.

Verbal Evidence

On October 11, 1992, a woman claiming to be Sister Lucy participated in a videotaped interview. In 1993, she was interviewed again and asked to confirm what she said in the 1992 interview, which she did. Here are some of her statements from those interviews:

1) "World War II was a war of atheism, a devil's war, a war also against the Jews who continue to be a chosen people of God."

Not only is this historically inaccurate in regards to World War II, it is blatantly heretical and a complete contradiction to Catholic teaching and dogma. In other words, it's something the real Sister Lucy would *never* say.

Also consider this: We know that at the very first apparition on May 13, 1917, Our Lady promised Lucy she would go to Heaven. No one disputes that. So knowing that the Blessed Virgin promised Lucy she would go to Heaven, is it even remotely possible that the real Sister Lucy would commit mortal sin by uttering such heretical words, words that would separate her from the Catholic Church and condemn her soul to eternity in the fires of hell?

No, it is not possible.

Doing so would be a slap in the face to the Mother of God, a mockery of the Holy Mother's promise.

You can say the same thing about the impostor Sister Lucy's public attendance at a non-Catholic and invalid New Mass in the year 2000.

Catholics are forbidden to attend non-Catholic services. The New Mass is not Catholic and thus it is a mortal sin for Catholics to attend. Would the real Sister Lucy dare to commit such an act after being told by Our Lady that she was going to Heaven? We know the Mother of God doesn't lie, so how can the real Sister Lucy commit these acts of mortal sin and still go to Heaven?

The answer is she can't.

(Note: If you are unaware that the New Mass is not Catholic and therefore a mortal sin for Catholics to attend, I urge you to read the book *The Truth about What Really Happened to the Catholic Church after Vatican II* and to visit the websites www.MostHolyFamilyMonastery.com and www.VaticanCatholic.com. Do it today. You'll find a wealth of documentation at those sources.)

You could make the argument that Sister Lucy could indeed commit mortal sin and still go to Heaven as long as she went to confession and/or received the Last Rites. For that to happen, Sister Lucy would have to receive those sacraments from a validly ordained priest, otherwise they wouldn't count.

If the real Sister Lucy, a public figure known throughout the world, did indeed commit the mortal sins of heresy and attendance at a non-Catholic service, and then received confession from a validly ordained priest, the priest likely would have told her, as part of her penance, to publicly renounce those sins. But that never happened, did it?

As for the Last Rites, when the impostor Sister Lucy died in 2005, there weren't many validly ordained priests around, so it's doubtful that even if that was the real Sister Lucy, which we know it wasn't, she would have received the last rights from a validly ordained priest.

There's also the issue of character. We know that Sister Lucy had great love and devotion to the Blessed Mother. Is it in Sister Lucy's character to cause such immense pain to the Blessed Mother's Immaculate Heart by performing public acts of mortal sin?

No, it is not.

Jesus is merciful, but when his Holy Mother promises someone they will go to Heaven, and then that same someone mocks and flaunts that promise by committing acts of mortal sin, it's treading on thin ice. Is it in Lucy's character to behave like this?

No, it is not.

Anyone who believes that Sister Lucy was not replaced with an impostor must therefore also believe that Sister Lucy publicly mocked the Blessed Virgin by committing outrageous acts of mortal sin, yet still went to Heaven. Either that or they believe the Blessed Virgin lied and Sister Lucy is not in Heaven. So which is it? It can't be both.

Finally, there's the question of whether someone that consciously planned to commit mortal sins of heresy and attendance of a non-Catholic service with the plan to confess them later would be forgiven. Padre Pio, a Catholic priest who was blessed with the grace to read souls, called this a sin against God's mercy.

A woman once came to Padre Pio and inquired about the state of her husband's soul. Even though the man confessed and received the last Sacraments before his death, Padre Pio told the woman that her husband's soul was condemned forever. Padre Pio added, "He was also a sinner against God's mercy, because he said he always wanted to have a share of the good things in life and then have time to be converted to God."

If Sister Lucy was not replaced with an impostor and really did commit these acts of mortal sin with the sly intention to confess them just before she died, isn't that also a sin against God's mercy? Would she then go to Heaven?

For Sister Lucy to engage in this kind of behavior, to commit multiple acts of mortal sin over a period of decades from the 1960s until her alleged death in 2005 with the plan to confess them all on her deathbed and somehow sneak into Heaven just before she died would be like playing Russian

Roulette with her eternal salvation on the line. It is so out of place with the character of the real Sister Lucy that it is simply inconceivable.

When you consider the multi-year span of these acts of mortal sin, it also becomes clear that the person committing them exhibited absolutely no remorse at all. That makes it even more incredulous that the real Sister Lucy was committing these sins and then going to confession.

Here's another statement from the 1992-93 interviews:

2) "He that is not with the Pope is not with God."

This actually contradicts her earlier statement that Jews "continue to be a chosen people of God." It's also worth noting that at the time this statement was made in 1992, the heretical Karol Wojtyla (John Paul II) was claiming to be the pope. The statement, "He that is not with the Pope is not with God," said at this time implies allegiance to Karol Wojtyla, a wicked and heretical antipope, something the real Sister Lucy would never do.

That John Paul II is wicked is easily confirmed by his numerous heresies and acts of apostasy:

John Paul II taught that those outside of the Catholic Church can be saved.

John Paul II taught that non-Christian religions, which would include both Wicca (Witchcraft) and Satanism, were inspired by the Holy Ghost.

John Paul II taught that every man is God: "You are the Christ, the Son of the Living God." The Bible says this is the sign of the antichrist.

John Paul II referred to Buddha as "Lord Buddha" and bowed before a statue of Buddha in a Buddhist temple.

John Paul II organized a World Day of Prayer for Peace attended by the leaders of dozens of false religions.

John Paul II prayed with Satanists and participated in voodoo ceremonies. (Yes, he did. On August 8, 1985 and February 4, 1993.)

John Paul II invited Satanists to pray at the Vatican and removed or covered all crucifixes so they would not be seen.

John Paul II kissed the Koran.

John Paul II participated in Jewish services.

And on and on. Bear in mind, this is only a partial list of the heresies and acts of apostasy committed by John Paul II. A full list would require at least ten pages. For more information on this topic visit www.VaticanCatholic.com or www.MostHolyFamilyMonastery.com.

That John Paul II is an antipope can be confirmed by the simple fact that heretics cease to be pope and cannot be elected pope. In fact, heretics automatically excommunicate themselves from the Church.

In the words of the Catholic Encyclopedia, 1914: "The pope himself, if notoriously guilty of heresy, would cease to be pope because he would cease to be a member of the Church."

This teaching of the Catholic Church therefore declares that John XXIII, Paul VI, John Paul I, John Paul II, Benedict XVI, and Francis are all antipopes.

Put that in your pipe and smoke it.

Here's another statement from the interview:

3) "God condemns no one to hell."

This is another heretical statement and a mockery of the First Secret of Fatima: the vision of hell that Our Lady gave to Lucy, Francisco and Jacinta. The real Sister Lucy, who saw hell with her own eyes, would not say this.

That God does indeed condemn people to hell is confirmed in Luke 12:5 "But I will shew you whom you shall fear: Fear ye him who, after he has killed, hath power to cast into hell. Yea, I say to you: Fear him."

4) "The Third Secret is not intended to be revealed. It was only intended for the Pope and the immediate church hierarchy."

This statement contradicts everything the real Sister Lucy said prior to 1960 concerning the Third Secret, including what she told Father Fuentes in her 1957 interview.

Anyone who believes these statements from the 1992-93 interviews were made by the real Sister Lucy needs to have their head examined.

Written Evidence

In 2001, a book entitled *Calls From the Message of Fatima* was published with Sister Lucy listed as the author. Even a cursory read of the book makes it obvious that it was not written by the same Sister Lucy who wrote her memoirs in 1935, 1937, and 1941. That observation is based on motive, content and style. Let's start with style.

An author's writing style is individual and identifiable, almost like a fingerprint. *Calls From the Message of Fatima* contains an entirely different rhythm, different sentence structure, different composition from the real Sister Lucy's memoirs. It has none of the mystery, none of the mystical reverence, none of the profound insight into Catholic teaching that the earlier book contains. It's clear to anyone with a trained eye that the two books were not authored by the same person.

What's even worse is the content. The book is a collection of Bible quotes peppered with vague, feel-good platitudes about love and spirituality. It contains no practical advice or teaching. Instead, everything is left blank for the reader to fill in with his or her own interpretation. Passages like: "The secret of happiness is love!" None of the Bible quotes in the book come from the Douay-Rheims Bible, which is the version the real Sister Lucy would have used.

The book contains heretical statements, such as this one:

"Everyone is obliged to be holy, even those who have no faith. Obviously, in the case of those who have no faith, the holiness will be that dictated by their own conscience, and there will be no supernatural merit because they will not have the fundamental reason that gives value to true holiness: 'to be holy because God is holy,' namely the desire to be holy in order to please God, to become like God, to do his Will, to give pleasure to God and prove to Him how much we love Him.

"As I was saying, those who do not have the happiness of possessing the gift of faith are also bound to become holy by a dictate of human conscience: for the same reason we say that even without knowing God those who fulfill the natural law can be saved, as St. Paul tells us."

Did you catch that?

In the last sentence, she writes that those who don't know God, those without the true Catholic Faith, can be saved. Would the real Sister Lucy dare to write something as heretical as this?

Elsewhere in the book the author claims to have been asked many times, "How are we to know the true Church of Christ?" She then says she doesn't know the answer. Sister

Lucy, of all people, doesn't know the answer? Sister Lucy, who knew her catechism at age six, who met the Mother of God at age ten, who saw a vision of hell and was present for the Miracle of the Sun, who saw Saint Joseph, Our Lady of Sorrows and Our Lady of Mount Carmel, and she doesn't know the answer? It is inconceivable that the real Sister Lucy wrote those words.

Finally, there's the question of motive. Sister Lucy has spent her entire adult life as a cloistered nun, hidden behind convent walls, inaccessible to the world. In her memoirs she states several times that she would prefer to remain anonymous and not to write them, that the only reason she is writing them is out of obedience:

> "I would like to ask just one favor. If Your Excellency should publish anything of what I have just written, would you do it in such a way that no mention whatsoever is made of my poor and miserable self. I must confess, moreover, that if it were to come to my knowledge that Your Excellency had burnt this account, without even reading it, I would be very glad indeed, since I wrote it solely out of obedience to the will of our Good God, as made known to me through the express will of Your Excellency."

That's the real Sister Lucy right there. She wants nothing to do with the world. All she wants is to be left alone. Are we to believe that suddenly, seemingly out of the blue and now in her nineties, she decides to write a book? A book that no one is asking her to write; a book that doesn't read like it was written by her at all, a book that contains heretical statements, a book that just happens to coincide with the watered-down, non-Catholic teachings of the Vatican II counterfeit church? Give me a break.

Calls From the Message of Fatima was not written by the real Sister Lucy. If you own a copy, I suggest you burn it or trash it. Don't give it away.

The Lies Just Keep on Coming

In 2007, "Cardinal" Tarcisio Bertone came out with a book entitled *The Last Secret of Fatima*. On page 80, he claims he asked Sister Lucy why the Third Secret was not to be read until the year 1960, and that she replied, "It was a decision that I took on my own initiative."

This is a complete contradiction to everything the real Sister Lucy said prior to 1960. Sister Lucy told Canon Barthas in 1946 that the secret was to be revealed in 1960, "Because the Blessed Virgin wishes it so." Other witnesses said the same thing.

Bertone could be making the story up, but it's still a bold-faced lie. We know the real Sister Lucy wouldn't lie like that, so either the impostor Sister Lucy or Bertone is lying.

On page 34 of his book, Bertone talks about antipope John Paul II's attempted high-jacking of the Rosary by initiating his own set of mysteries, and claims Sister Lucy was "overjoyed" by it. That is as big of a lie as you'll ever hear anywhere. The real Sister Lucy would be aghast at the idea of anyone other than the Virgin Mary herself changing the Rosary.

(Note: It's worth noting that John Paul II's attempt to hijack the Rosary is an old Communist trick. They float idea bubbles up to see if they pop, and then act according to the reaction. If antipope John Paul II's introduction of the "luminous mysteries" hadn't failed, it would have likely led to more attempts to update and subsequently destroy the Rosary. By now, we'd have seven completely different sets of mysteries, one for each day of the week. Antipope Francis floated his own idea bubble up recently when he suggested rewriting the Our Father prayer.)

On page 85 of Bertrone's book, the person interviewing him makes the astounding claim that Sister Lucy kept a *secret diary!* We are told that in this secret diary, in the year 1955, Sister Lucy wrote the following about World War II:

". . . in the sense that it would be an atheistic war that attempted to exterminate Judaism, which gave the world Jesus Christ, Our Lady, the Apostles, who transmitted the Word of God and the gift of faith, hope, and charity. The Jews are God's elect people, whom he chose from the beginning: 'Salvation is of the Jews.' "

Sound familiar? The first and last sentences are an almost word-for-word recitation of what the impostor Sister Lucy said at her 1992-93 interviews. It's as if a writer came up with the words and the impostor Sister Lucy memorized them. These are words that will send a person straight to hell, words that the real Sister Lucy would never write or say. No Christian would. Would you?

On page 135 of Bertone's book, the interviewer states that these same heretical words were in "Sister Lucy's" 2006 memoirs, *Come vedo il Messaggio di Fatima nel corso del tempo e degli avvenimenti*, published posthumously.

Now it's really sounding like a scriptwriter penned these words for someone to memorize and recite.

Knowing what we know about Sister Lucy's character, is it at all plausible that she would speak or write words such as these?

We have already determined that it is not plausible.

In her memoirs, Sister Lucy informs us that she knew her catechism so well at age six that she was allowed to take her first Communion a year earlier than required. Does it make sense that someone so inflamed with a love for the Catholic Faith, someone who met and spoke with the Mother of God and was promised Heaven herself, someone who became a nun and continued to express deep concern for the

37

fate of humanity and the souls of so many poor sinners would, very late in life, become such a notorious sinner?

At this point, you would not be surprised to learn that on page 123 of his book, Bertone brags of committing an act of total apostasy when he attended a mosque with antipope Benedict, where they both bowed their heads and prayed.

It's enough to make a person puke.

Put Yourself in Sister Lucy's Shoes

If *you* were served Holy Communion by the Guardian Angel of Portugal; if *you* were visited by the Virgin Mary and shown a frightening vision of hell; if *you* were entrusted with three secrets, secrets so grave you refused to reveal them even under the threat of death; if *you* had spent decades living as a cloistered nun; if *you* had experienced all of those things would you suddenly turn on a dime late in life and start spouting off the heresy that is attributed to Sister Lucy after the year 1960? Would you, for no apparent reason, begin committing multiple acts of mortal sin by uttering and writing such heretical words and by supporting the non-Catholic and invalid New Mass and its succession of antipopes? Would you, again for no apparent reason, contradict all of your earlier statements and written words regarding the Third Secret of Fatima?

I think you know the answer.

The question is, are you brave enough and clearheaded enough to admit the obvious? Most people aren't. Most people find it easier to believe the statements of known liars rather than expend a few brain cells to think for themselves. They actually prefer being duped. Life is more comfortable that way.

Now in fairness to the duped, many of them have never seen the comparison photos of Sister Lucy and her impostor before. Many of them may not even know what Fatima is. I've talked to people who call themselves Catholic and they tell me they've never even heard of Fatima. It was never taught to them. But you know what Fatima is and you've seen the photos. You can no longer plead ignorance on this issue.

We know that Our Lady promised Sister Lucy she would go to Heaven. No one disputes that. We also know that after the year 1960, the person calling herself Sister Lucy committed multiple acts of mortal sin, including heresy and attendance at a non-Catholic service. No one disputes that either. Therefore, anyone who believes Sister Lucy was not replaced with an impostor must also believe she was a total scoundrel who publicly mocked Our Lady's promise of going to Heaven. And yet, knowing that Our Lady promised Sister Lucy she would go to Heaven, we know that is not possible.

We've now covered three vital areas of evidence:

1) Comparison photos of Sister Lucy and her impostor. 2) Statements made or attributed to Sister Lucy. 3) Books

written or alleged to have been written by Sister Lucy. At this point, it's clear we are dealing with a multitude of lies, and that the real Sister Lucy was replaced by an impostor.

Having said that, I know how frightening some of this material can be the first time you hear it. Acknowledging that Sister Lucy was replaced by an impostor means the institution you put your faith in, the "church" you thought was real and in which you entrusted the fate of your eternal soul, is in actuality an evil and criminal enterprise. It means that if they lied to you about this, then they probably lied to you about everything else too. That's pretty scary stuff.

I also know that a lot of people reading this are so used to having other people do their thinking for them (not you, of course) that they are incapable of making up their own mind on any subject. For those reasons, I recommend once again that you visit the website www.SisterLucyTruth.org. There you'll find facial recognition reports, plastic surgery reports, dental reports, handwriting analysis, and more photos.

Study the information on Dr. Chojnowski's website. If you still don't believe that Sister Lucy was replaced with an impostor then, quite frankly, there's nothing more that I or anyone else can do to help you. You've made up your mind and no amount of facts, evidence or conclusive proof is going to change it.

Chapter 3

Top-4 Arguments of an Impostor Denier

Incredible as it may seem, there are many people who, after looking at the photographs of the real Sister Lucy and her impostor, and after reading through all of the other available evidence, still deny what their own eyes are telling them. Their reaction is always the same: they frown, give their head a little shake, and then insist that the women in the two photographs are the same person. These impostor deniers have four main arguments they use to support their position. Let's examine their top-4 arguments.

Argument #1) *The pictures portray the same woman. They look different because Sister Lucy has aged.*

Of all the arguments put forth by those who refuse to acknowledge the truth, this is the most ridiculous, and I can prove it to you in less than 60 seconds. Find some pictures of your parents, your grandparents, or even yourself that are spaced 20, 30, 40 or more years apart, look at them, and what do you see?

I'll tell you what you see: You see the same person, only older.

Hair may have turned gray, or be missing completely, weight may have been gained or lost, but the eyes, the shape of the face, and the facial structure are all still the same. You can tell it's the same person.

Look at pictures of Ronald Reagan at age 35 and then in his 80s and 90s. You can easily see it's the same guy.

Look at pictures of Donald Trump, aged 35 and today. Same guy.

Look at pictures of John Wayne, aged 35 and in his 70s. Same guy.

Look at pictures of Paul Newman, aged 35 and before he died in his 80s. Same guy.

Look at pictures of Anthony Hopkins, aged 35 and today at age 83. Same guy.

Look at all the pictures you want. In every case, you can see very clearly that it's the same person, only older.

But those are all men, you say? Okay, let's look at some women.

Look at pictures of Brigitte Bardot in her 20s and today in her 80s. She has aged, sure, and she has gained a lot of weight, but you can clearly see she has the same nose, the same chin, the same eyes and the same eyebrow shape. You can tell it's her.

Look at pictures of Bette Davis in her 20's and in her 70s. She also aged, but her mouth, the shape of her face, and especially her eyes are exactly the same.

Look at pictures of Katherine Hepburn in her 20s and in her 80s. Same person.

Look at pictures of Mae West aged 37 and aged 67. Same person.

Keep looking. You'll see the same thing with every person you choose. Even with women who have succumbed to the horror of plastic surgery, you can tell it's the same person.

Now look again at the photos on the back cover of this book. You can clearly see that everything is different: the nose, the eyes, the teeth, the shape of the smile and eyebrows, everything. The entire facial structure is different and so is the skin color. Sister Lucy's olive-colored complexion has inexplicably turned pale white. This change in skin color is even more evident in the color film that was shot when the impostor Sister Lucy met with John Paul II in 1991. Her skin looks white as a ghost.

If the pictures on the back cover of this book are both honest portrayals of the real Sister Lucy, then she is the first person in the history of the world whose dimples have disappeared and whose entire facial structure and skin color have changed over the course of aging; the first person in history whose facial shape changed from oval to round as she got older. Isn't that amazing?

Pictures don't lie. People do.

Argument #2) *The pictures portray the same woman.*
They look different because Sister Lucy had plastic surgery
and had her teeth fixed and/or replaced with dentures.

Of all the arguments put forth by those who refuse to
acknowledge the truth, this is the most laughable. The idea
that Sister Lucy, a nun who rejected the world and all
worldly pursuits, would resort to cosmetic surgery is simply
absurd. She spent decades as a cloistered nun. Does anyone
really think she would suddenly develop issues of vanity and
want to cosmetically change her appearance? For whom
would she be doing this, the fellow nuns in her convent?

Did Sister Lucy, way back in 1960, resort to lightening
her skin, a la Michael Jackson? Did Sister Lucy have her
dimples surgically removed? Did Sister Lucy somehow,
someway, have the shape of her entire face changed?

Even if Sister Lucy did cosmetically alter her appearance,
there would still be some resemblance to her former self. She
wouldn't look completely different.

Argument #3) *The pictures portray the same woman. I*
know this to be a fact, because the Vatican says so.

Of all the arguments put forth by those who refuse to
acknowledge the truth, this is the saddest. If you're an

impostor denier, because the Vatican tells you these pictures portray the same woman, let me ask you this: If you had a friend or family member who lied to your face and you caught them in the lie, would you believe anything they said after that?

Most likely not, but suppose you did and then you caught them in a second lie, and a third lie, and a fourth lie, would you still believe anything they said? Again, most likely not, although some would say it depends on the seriousness of the lie. Fair enough. Let's say the lie had to do with child molestation. Your friend or family member said they didn't do it, but mountains of evidence and thousands of eyewitnesses all said they did. Would you still believe your friend or family member?

What if your friend or family member was caught red-handed molesting children and lied to you about it not once, not twice, but literally dozens of times? What if they were convicted in court of child molestation after lying about it, not once, not twice, but literally dozens of times? Would you believe anything that person told you ever again?

The post Vatican II counterfeit church is your lying friend or family member.

When a witness lies in court, all of their previous testimony gets called into question. The Vatican II counterfeit church has been lying about their participation in child rape and molestation for over 50 years, yet millions of dull-witted impostor deniers continue to lap up their lies.

(Note: The massive sex abuse scandal that has ensnared the entire Novus Ordo Church—the child rapes, the child molestations, all of it—did not occur prior to Vatican II. It is a manifestation of the counterfeit church's abandonment of the true Catholic faith. And this abandonment of the true Catholic faith is a vital component of the Third Secret of Fatima, as we'll see a little later.)

As for obedience to the pope, that only applies to real popes, not antipopes. We've already quoted the words of the Catholic Encyclopedia of 1914: "The pope himself, if notoriously guilty of heresy, would cease to be pope because he would cease to be a member of the Church."

Notice that not only does a heretic cease to hold the office of pope they also cease to be Catholic. To recognize such a person as a true pope is a grave sin. Every claimant to the office of pope after Pius XII has committed acts of heresy and apostasy. Hence, they are all antipopes.

Obedience to the pope is the last refuge of the impostor denier. Anyone choosing that line of defense is really lost.

Argument #4) *If Sister Lucy was replaced with an impostor, the other nuns in her convent would have noticed.*

They did notice. The zenit news agency of Rome reported on September 25, 2007 that guests at a reception for "Cardinal" Tarcisio Bertone's book *The Last Secret of Fatima* were treated to a video about Sister Lucy, narrated by her

Carmelite Superior for 28 years, Sister Maria Celine. In the video, Sister Lucy's own superior says, "When I entered it took me eight days to recognize Sister Lucia. When one of the sisters asked me: "Mother, should I bring you a piece of bread to eat tonight?' I said to myself that this could not be Sister Lucia. And yet it was her."

So here we have the new Mother Superior, arriving at the convent of the most famous nun in the world; someone whose pictures the new Mother Superior had seen for years, someone the whole world was familiar with, and it took Sister Maria *eight days* to recognize her.

The impostor Sister Lucy died in 2005, so if Sister Maria Celine was with her for 28 years, she arrived at the convent around the year 1977, when the real Sister Lucy would have been around 70-years-old, approximately ten years older than the woman on the right of the two comparison photos on the front cover of this book.

That's the person Sister Maria met and was unable to recognize as the real Sister Lucy for eight days, despite living with her and seeing her in person. Yet how many people look at the two photographs and immediately declare them to be the same woman, despite no physical resemblance at all?

Sister Maria's words are very telling: "I said to myself that this could not be Sister Lucia. And yet it was her." Like so many others, she couldn't believe what her own eyes were showing her. Like so many others, she talked herself into believing what she knew wasn't true.

To sum up then, we have a Vatican that has raped and molested children for the last fifty-plus years; openly lied about it the entire time; accused their victims of lying; obstructed justice and covered up their crimes by shuffling known pedophile 'priests' from one parish to another; and now they're telling us that two women who look nothing at all alike are the same person. Do you believe them?

Chapter 4

What Happened to the Real Sister Lucy?

Now that we've established that Sister Lucy was replaced by an impostor, the question becomes, what happened to the real Sister Lucy?

There are only three possible answers: 1) Sister Lucy died of natural causes sometime around the year 1960. 2) Sister Lucy was locked away somewhere around the year 1960. 3) Sister Lucy was murdered.

If Sister Lucy died of natural causes, it slightly lessens the gravity of the crime involved, but it doesn't lessen the gravity of the sin. Replacing Sister Lucy with an impostor after her natural death is still a massive deception whose end result has been and continues to be the condemning of millions of souls to hell.

Think about it. By giving the world an impostor Sister Lucy, the Vatican II counterfeit church was able to hide the true contents of the Third Secret and dupe millions of people into accepting the non-Catholic and invalid New Mass.

That's quite an accomplishment. Catholics are forbidden to attend non-Catholic services. When the Catholic Latin Mass was replaced with the New Mass, it ceased being Catholic. Thus, anyone attending the New Mass is committing mortal sin and condemning their soul to hell.

The people behind the deception actually installed two impostors, one for Sister Lucy and one for the true Mass.

(Note: Once again, if this is your first time hearing that the New Mass is invalid and you find that information shocking, then I urge you to research the issue yourself. Failure to do so could result in your own soul being condemned to hell for all eternity.)

Regarding the fate of the real Sister Lucy, out of the three possible scenarios that could have occurred, the least likely one is her dying of natural causes.

For starters, it's highly coincidental that the real Sister Lucy would have died of natural causes at the exact same time that the Third Secret was supposed to be released in the year 1960 and only a few short years before the non-Catholic and invalid New Mass was introduced. Sure, it's possible, but it's not very likely.

More importantly, the replacement of Sister Lucy with an impostor requires planning, as well as the grooming of someone suitable to replace her. The replacement would have to be someone who either physically resembled the real Sister Lucy or who could be made to physically resemble her through plastic surgery. Also it would have to be someone who spoke Portuguese or who could learn to speak Portuguese. As we can see, the woman they chose to play the part looks nothing at all like the real Sister Lucy, but the fact that she's the one that was picked shows you just how difficult the task was.

The most likely scenario is that several women were considered for the job, groomed, and had their appearances altered in order to play the impostor, and then the best of the bunch was chosen. But what if something happened to her? The only logical way to carry out an operation like this would be to have several potential impostors ready to go at any time. All of that requires time and planning. It's not something that could have been put into motion on the spot, such as the day after Sister Lucy died of natural causes.

If the perpetrators *knew* Sister Lucy was dying, then maybe they could have come up with a plan and started recruiting potential impostors, but then what if Sister Lucy's illness dragged on? After all the planning and preparation, do you think anyone evil enough to deceive millions of people into condemning themselves to hell would just patiently sit back and wait for poor Sister Lucy to die? Also, if Sister Lucy became seriously ill, news may have leaked out. After all, she was the most famous nun in the world, a household name among Catholics. Her illness certainly would have been newsworthy.

We can safely say that Sister Lucy dying of natural causes is the least likely of three possible scenarios.

The Nun in the Iron Mask

The second possible answer to the question of what happened to the real Sister Lucy is that she was locked away someplace where no one could see her while an impostor usurped her identity. Sort of like the story of *The Man in the Iron Mask*.

I can't say for sure that this didn't happen. After all, it *is* possible. But what are the odds? Locking Sister Lucy away leaves open the possibility of detection and escape.

The first rule of any crime is to keep the number of participants and witnesses to a minimum. To imprison Sister Lucy would require guards, jailers and supervisors, any one of whom could spill the beans or help her escape.

Locking someone away like that is kidnapping, a serious crime, but in this case the kidnappers would have nothing to gain in terms of ransom money, so what would the point be? Why keep her alive?

If Sister Lucy was locked away it would have to be for life, otherwise she would talk as soon as she was released.

She would also have to be fed and cared for to some extent, which again expands the number of witnesses to the crime and adds to the expense. For all of these reasons and more, the idea that Sister Lucy was locked away and replaced with an impostor is highly unlikely.

If you eliminate the first two scenarios of what happened to the real Sister Lucy, that she died of natural causes or that she was hidden away and locked up someplace, the only remaining possibility is murder.

This is by far the most likely scenario. It pains me to write this, but the murder of Sister Lucy could have been performed quick and clean with a minimum of participants and witnesses, and then, if necessary, those participants and witnesses could likewise be eliminated.

You also have to ask yourself which scenario makes the most sense. When a criminal enterprise lies to the world and replaces someone with an impostor, what's the most likely outcome of the person who is replaced?

On page 552 of the book *The Truth about What Really Happened to the Catholic Church after Vatican II*, there is a startling revelation by the authors. They were contacted by a woman who comes from a family of 33rd degree Freemasons. The woman revealed that in 1958 she heard her family discussing how they had just recently murdered Sister Lucy.

Obviously, there's no way to prove whether this woman was telling the truth or not, but the authors of the book believed her, and the timing of the year 1958 aligns perfectly to when Sister Lucy was replaced. We have to admit that of the three possible scenarios involving the fate of the real Sister Lucy, the most likely scenario is murder.

Are you shocked? Saddened? If there's any consolation to such distressing news, we know that Sister Lucy was immediately taken to Heaven, as Our Lady promised she would be.

If murder and the use of impostors seems a little too James Bondish for you, be aware that the use of impostors and body doubles is a decades-old Communist trick.

It's well documented that Joseph Stalin had multiple body doubles. So did Winston Churchill and Sadam Hussein. I'm sure Putin in Russia has body doubles at his disposal.

We saw in the 2016 Presidential Election that Hillary Clinton has at least two body doubles, and we can see that our current fake president has at least three. So it's not nearly as farfetched as some people might think.

Sister Lucy's Death and False Apparitions

Over the last fifty or more years, a number of false apparitions have occurred around the world. Chief among these are the false apparitions of Bayside, New York and the false apparitions of Medjugorje, Bosnia.

These are exceedingly evil apparitions that are leading many souls to hell. They do that by conning their followers into accepting the heresies of Vatican II, which are contrary to the Catholic Faith.

An easy way to spot a false apparition is the presence of any message that contradicts Catholic teaching. The apparitions of Bayside and Medjugorje both contain the heretical message that those outside the Catholic Church can be saved. Since we know the Blessed Virgin would never say anything that contradicts Church teaching, we know that both of these apparitions are false.

At this point, we need no further proof that both Bayside and Medjugorje are false apparitions. However, the replacement of Sister Lucy with an impostor does provide us with even more evidence.

On June 18, 1986, the seer of Bayside reported this message:

> "I wish at this time, my children, to repeat again the need to write, to speak, to meet with the Holy Father in Rome, and plead with him to have Lucy come forward and tell the Third Secret word for word, as I give to you each evening in my appearances upon the grounds of Bayside, and Flushing Meadows."

This message contains two enormous "tells". First, we know that the real Sister Lucy either died or was locked away sometime around the year 1960. If that is the case, how is she going to "come forward" 26 years later and tell the Third Secret? This false apparition would have you believe that Sister Lucy was alive and well in 1986.

I know some of you don't want to hear this, because you're devoted to the Bayside apparitions, but facts are facts. We know that Sister Lucy was replaced with an impostor around the year 1960 and that she was almost certainly killed around the same time. All available evidence points to those conclusions.

As Sherlock Holmes would say, "When you remove the impossible, whatever remains, no matter how improbable, must be the truth." So if Sister Lucy was dead in 1986, then this message and the entire Bayside apparition is a lie.

Yes, it's possible that for 26 years, from 1960 until 1986, Sister Lucy was locked away someplace, as we've already discussed, but what are the odds? And if that was the case, why was no mention made of it in the Bayside message? If the real Sister Lucy was locked away, would it truly do any good, as the message implies, "to write, to speak, to meet with the Holy Father in Rome, and plead with him to have Lucy come forward and tell the Third Secret"? No, it wouldn't do any good.

If this were an authentic apparition, we would be told the truth, that Sister Lucy was replaced with an impostor.

There's another "tell" in this message from Bayside. It occurred in 1986 when John Paul II was occupying the Vatican. The Blessed Virgin would never refer to wicked antipope John Paul II as the "Holy Father."

So that's more proof that Bayside is a false apparition.

In the false apparitions of Medjugorje, it appears no mention of Sister Lucy is made at all. I did a search of Sister Lucy's name in a database of the messages and the results said there was no match.

If Medjugorje was a legitimate apparition, we would have surely been told much about Fatima, the Third Secret and the fate of Sister Lucy. Instead we get crickets.

We don't really need these additional proofs that Bayside and Medjugorje are false apparitions. We already know they are false, because they promote the heresy that those outside the Catholic Church can be saved. Catholic teaching and the Bible both maintain that no one outside the Catholic Church can be saved. Anyone who says otherwise, whether it's our current antipope or an apparition, is committing heresy.

St. Paul tells us in Galations 1:8:

"But though we, or an angel from heaven, preach a gospel to you besides that which we have preached to you, let him be anathema."

The word "anathema" means excommunicated. When any of the men who have claimed to be pope after Pius XII speak or write about those outside the Catholic Church being saved, as they have done many times, they are committing heresy. According to St. Paul they should be immediately excommunicated and that is also the teaching of the Church.

It's the same with any apparition.

The apparitions of Bayside and Medjugorje also advise their followers to attend the non-Catholic and invalid New Mass, which we know is a mortal sin. That is further proof that they are false apparitions.

If you've been a believer in Bayside or Medjugorje up until this time, there's no shame in admitting you've been duped. In fact, it's a sign of intelligence. We've all been duped at one time or another. The shame lies with those who have been duped, but are too stupid or too proud to admit it, which is an accurate description of the majority of the human race.

Chapter 5

Why was Sister Lucy Replaced?

Do you have a pretty good idea at this point why Sister Lucy had to be replaced? If not, consider the timing of her disappearance and her replacement with an impostor which we know occurred around the year 1960, along with what took place in the church after 1960 and what the impostor Sister Lucy did after 1960.

The 1960s gave us Vatican II, the non-Catholic and invalid New Mass, and an invalid ordination process for priests. It was an almost complete destruction of the Catholic Church. Would Sister Lucy have stood for such changes? No, she would not have. And because Sister Lucy was a public figure, her resistance to these changes could have influenced millions of people. Now do you see why she had to be eliminated and replaced with an impostor?

Sister Lucy's removal was a necessary step in order to implement the heretical changes of Vatican II. Not only that, but her approval was necessary, as well. That's why she had to be replaced with an impostor who could then feign acceptance of both Vatican II and the invalid New Mass.

Finally, there's the Third Secret. Rumors that it dealt with exactly these same issues made it something to be squelched. What better way to do that than by having an impostor Sister Lucy pretend to agree with the Vatican's false interpretation of the Third Secret?

And that's exactly what happened. The impostor Sister Lucy was trotted out and filmed receiving "communion" from John Paul II at a non-Catholic and invalid New Mass. She also confirmed the Vatican's phony interpretation of the Third Secret. For untold numbers of Catholics, seeing the impostor Sister Lucy agree with these changes and endorse the fake Third Secret convinced them to do the same.

If you're wondering how all of this could have taken place and why good people in the Church didn't put a stop to it, the answer is some good people did try to put a stop to it, but they were outnumbered and outmaneuvered by the massive Communist infiltration and subversion of the Catholic Church that began decades prior and was in full command by the year 1960. It was literally a Communist takeover.

Anyone who claims a Communist takeover of the Church "could never happen" is an idiot. It already *has* happened. To find out how and when this occurred, turn to the next chapter.

Chapter 6

The Communist Infiltration of the Church

"Yet the individual is handicapped by coming face to face with a conspiracy so monstrous he cannot believe it exists. The American mind simply has not come to a realization of the evil which has been introduced into our midst. It rejects even the assumption that human creatures could espouse a philosophy which must ultimately destroy all that is good and decent." —J. Edgar Hoover, *The Elks Magazine*, August 1956

When J. Edgar Hoover spoke those words back in 1956, he was referring to the massive Communist infiltration of the United States government that began near the turn of the century and accelerated immensely during the FDR, Truman and Eisenhower administrations, but he could just as easily have been talking about the Communist infiltration of the Catholic Church that was occurring at the same time. Today, both the United States government and the Catholic Church have been completely infiltrated, subverted and overthrown by Communism.

Manning Johnson

Manning Johnson was a Communist agent who left the Party and wrote a book about his experiences. Johnson's book, *Color, Communism and Common Sense* reads like it could have been written yesterday:

> "After two years of practical training and organizing street demonstrations, inciting mob violence, how to fight the police and how to politically 'throw a brick and hide,' I was ready, in the opinion of my leaders, for a top Communist school."

Sound familiar?

In 1953, Johnson testified to the House Un-American Committee about the massive Communist infiltration of the Church:

> "Briefly, the Communist Party is anti-religious. Communism and religion have nothing in common. Religion is the antithesis of Communism. Consequently, the Communists are unalterably

opposed to it, and their program calls for a ceaseless struggle or war to the complete extermination and extinction of religion from the face of the earth.

"Once the tactic of infiltrating religious organizations was set by the Kremlin, the actual mechanics of implementing the 'new line' was a question of following the general experiences of the living church movement in Russia where the Communists discovered that the destruction of religion could proceed much faster through infiltration of the Church by Communist agents operating within the Church itself.

"The Communist leadership in the United States realized that the infiltration tactic in this country would have to adapt itself to American conditions and the religious makeup peculiar to this country. In the earliest stages it was determined that with only small forces available it would be necessary to concentrate Communist agents in the seminaries and divinity schools. The practical conclusion, drawn by the Red leaders was that these institutions would make it possible for a small Communist minority to influence the ideology of future clergymen in the paths most conducive to Communist purposes.

"The plan was to make the seminaries the neck of a funnel through which thousands of potential clergymen would issue forth, carrying with them, in varying degrees, an ideology . . . which would aid in neutralizing the anti-Communist character of the Church.

"This policy was successful beyond even Communist expectations. The combination of Communist clergymen, clergymen with a pro-Communist ideology, plus thousands of clergymen who were sold the principle of considering causes as progressive, within 20 years, furnished the Soviet apparatus with a machine which was used as a religious cover for the overall Communist operation ranging from immediate demands to actually furnishing aid in espionage and outright treason."

Manning Johnson was talking about the 1930s and 40s. That's how far back the subversion goes.

Bella Dodd

Bella Dodd was a 21-year member of the Communist Party USA who used her Communist connections to become the head of the New York State Teachers' Union. (Some things never change.)

Dodd wrote about her experiences in her book *School of Darkness*. Like Manning Johnson, she also testified before the House Un-American Committee where she spoke of the mass Communist infiltration of the country's teachers' unions throughout New York and the rest of the country.

Dodd was baptized Catholic as a child. After she left the Communist Party she returned to the Church. During that period, she went on a lecture tour. She is reported to have said at one of her public lectures, "In the 1930s, we put eleven hundred men into the priesthood in order to destroy the Church from within. . . . Right now they are in the highest places, and they are working to bring about change in order that the Catholic Church will no longer be effective against communism."

That was almost a hundred years ago. Multiply Bella Dodd and Manning Johnson by dozens of other Communist agents around the world, each one training scores of men to enter the Catholic Church in order to subvert it from within, add a century of time for them all to do their dirty work and spawn others to replace them, and what do you get? You get the corrupt, non-Catholic, counterfeit church that occupies the Vatican today.

A church that abandoned the Holy Sacrifice of the Mass and replaced it with a Protestant service; a church that rapes and molests innocent children by the thousands and then lies to cover up its crimes; a church led by a series of heretical, non-Catholic antipopes dating back to late 1950s; a church that has completely abandoned traditional Catholic teaching and dogma. That's what you get. It's literally a separate religion from the Catholic Church.

Surprised? You shouldn't be. The Catholic Church has always been the #1 enemy of Communism and the New World Order. It's a war that has been waging for centuries.

In Dodd's lectures, she repeatedly said the Catholic Church is the only religion truly feared by the Communist Party, because the Catholic Church is Communism's only effective opponent, the only force capable of stopping it.

Christian Rakovsky and the Unknown Light

In 1938, at the same time that Bella Dodd, Manning Johnson and their fellow agents were training thousands of men to infiltrate and destroy the Catholic Church from within, Christian Rakovsky, a Freemason and one of the founders of Soviet Bolshevism, was arrested and interrogated by the all-seeing Stalinist Secret Police (NKVD).

Rakovsky admitted at his interrogation that the Catholic Church was Communism's #1 enemy and therefore must be destroyed. He convinced the Soviet high command to make a pact with Germany for a double invasion of Poland as a pretext for England, France and the United States to declare war on Germany in order to further Communism in Europe.

Rakovsky gave his interrogator three reasons to do this:

1) To destroy Germany for having the audacity to print their own money and to prevent their example from spreading to other nations. According to Rakovsky, this was

Germany's cardinal sin; the primary reason why they were targeted for destruction.

2) To stamp out Germany's nationalistic spirit and prevent it from spreading to other countries.

3) To weaken and destroy the Catholic Church.

Here are Rakovsky's own words from his tape-recorded interrogation reprinted in the book *Red Symphony* by Dr. J. Landowsky:

> "Hitler, this uneducated and elementary man, has restored thanks to his natural intuition and even against the technical opinion of Schacht, an economic system of a very dangerous kind . . . he took over for himself the privilege of manufacturing money . . . he has by means of magic, as it were, radically eliminated unemployment among more than seven million technicians and workers.
>
> "Are you capable of imagining what would have come of this system if it had infected a number of other states . . . This is very serious. Much more so than all the external and cruel factors in National Socialism . . . There is only one solution—war.
>
> ". . . in Russia there was no real nationalism . . . the need for the destruction of nationalism is alone worth a war in Europe.
>
> "We have yet another reason, a religious one. Communism cannot be the victor if it will not have

suppressed the still living Christianity. History speaks very clearly about this: the permanent revolution required centuries in order to achieve its first partial victory by means of the creation of the first split in Christendom. Christianity is our only real enemy."

In return for helping to create a pretext for the Allies to attack Germany, Rakovsky, on behalf of his employers, promised the Soviets half of Europe at the conclusion of the war. When his interrogators expressed skepticism, Rakovsky advised them to contact Joseph Davies, the U.S. Ambassador in Moscow at the time to confirm everything he'd just told them. The rest, as they say, is history.

Germany and Russia both invaded Poland—Germany to rescue its own citizens who were being raped, mutilated and murdered by Polish terrorists in the Danzig Corridor, and Russia to seize territory—and then England and France ignored Russia and declared war on Germany.

It's worth noting that Rakovsky admitted in his interview how the enemies of the Church had a hand in duping Martin Luther and engineering the Protestant Reformation.

It's also worth noting that Rakovsky's interrogation began just after midnight in the early morning hour of January 26, 1938, at the same time that the skies of Europe were illuminated by an unknown light. Our Lady of Fatima told the young seers on July 13, 1917, that this unknown light would be a sign from Heaven that God intended to punish the world for its crimes by means of war, hunger, and persecution of the Church and of the Holy Father.

This unknown light that inflamed the skies of Europe was visible on January 25, 1938 from 6:30 to 9:30 PM. In Moscow time, where Rakovsky's interrogation took place, the time was 9:30 PM to 12:30 AM. As this sign from Heaven illuminated the skies of Europe, the interrogation of Christian Rakovsky and the plans to begin World War II were just getting underway.

The Catholic Gazette

In February of 1936, the London edition of the *Catholic Gazette,* an official Catholic organ, published an article about the Freemasonic infiltration of the Church.

The article contained the minutes of several Freemasonic meetings in which the plans for the subversion and takeover of the Church were discussed. Here are some quotes:

"We still have a long way to go before we can overthrow our main opponent: the Catholic Church. We must always bear in mind that the Catholic Church is the only institution which has stood, and which will, as long as it remains in existence, stand in our way.

"We have induced some of our children to join the Catholic body, with the explicit intimation that they should work in a still more efficient way for the disintegration of the Catholic Church, by creating scandals within her.

"We can boast of being the creators of the Reformation!

"We are grateful to Protestants for their loyalty to our wishes, although most of them are, in the sincerity of their faith, unaware of their loyalty to us. We are grateful to them for the wonderful help they are giving us in our fight against the stronghold of Christian Civilization . . .

". . . let us therefore encourage in a still more violent way the hatred of the world against the Catholic Church . . . Let us, above all, make it impossible for Christians outside the Catholic Church to be reunited with that Church, or for non-Christians to join the Church, otherwise the greatest obstruction to our domination will be strengthened and all our work undone."

Once again, we see a frank acknowledgement that the Catholic Church is the #1 enemy of the forces of evil. We also see confirmation of Rakovsky's claim, that these enemies of the Church were instrumental in duping Martin Luther and instigating the Protestant Reformation, an event that has condemned literally billions of souls to hell over the last 500 years.

The Church Today

We've just covered four impeccable sources, all from times past, confirming independently of each other a plot to destroy the Catholic Church.

They describe the situation as it was occurring *then*. You don't have to imagine how bad things are *today*. All you have to do is observe what has occurred and what is presently occurring. We have a non-Catholic and invalid New Mass; invalid ordination rites for the priesthood (anyone ordained after 1968 is not a valid priest); an unbroken line of heretical antipopes after Pius XII; child molestation and sex scandals in parishes across the globe; "priests" and "bishops" condoning abominable sins and preaching acceptance of false religions. In other words, the Church has been subverted.

Even if someone is too dense to acknowledge these facts, they can't deny what's staring them right in the face: "Catholic" schools flying the rainbow flag and teaching sex initiation; antipopes denying the existence of hell, celebrating pagan religions and declaring that followers of pagan religions are saved; "bishops" embracing sodomy and homosexuality; "priests" coming out as gay; "nuns" coming out as lesbians and feminists and promoting abortion, and on and on.

Yet there are those today who still refuse to see; who continue to deny; who shrug and say, "That's not enough."

If everything listed above is not enough, then I don't know what else Communist subversion looks like. Just how much more proof does a denialist need in order to be convinced? Bolshevik soldiers in fur hats goose-stepping down the street? "Catholic" schools and churches hoisting the hammer and sickle flag? Some people are so lost they will never wake up.

Jesus said, "By their fruits, you will know them." The fruits are there for all to see, but the willfully blind refuse to acknowledge what their own eyes are showing them.

If all this comes as a shock to you, it shouldn't. What we are living in now are the end times as prophesized in the final book of the Bible, The Apocalypse, and as Our Lady of La Salette foretold when she said, "Rome will lose the Faith and become the seat of the antichrist."

Don't make the same mistake that so many others do. They cite the words of Our Lord when he said in Matthew 16:18: "And I say to thee: That thou art Peter, and upon this rock I will build my church. And the gates of hell shall not prevail against it." They then use this quote to deny everything taking place before their eyes. But the existence of a counterfeit church does not deny the words of Jesus.

The Catholic Church remains, and always will remain, but not in the Vatican or in the physical buildings currently occupied by the counterfeit church. The Catholic Church today exists in small handfuls of faithful followers, and you won't find them in any of the churches or schools that call themselves Catholic.

I'm one of those faithful and traditional Catholics. You, reading this, might be one. There are others like us, but not many. There might be ten thousand true Catholics left in the world today, maybe twenty thousand.

Here's a good way to look at it: Suppose you had a neighbor named John Smith, and suppose you kidnapped him and moved your cousin into John Smith's house. Your cousin could then claim he was John Smith, and he could point to the fact that he's living in John Smith's house and wearing John Smith's clothes to prove his case. If he was clever enough, he could convince the neighbors, the legal authorities and anyone else who might ask that he really was John Smith. But none of those things would make him John Smith. He would forever remain an impostor. Meanwhile, the real John Smith would still be alive.

That's the situation with the Catholic Church today. Usurpers have taken over the buildings and physical structures of the Catholic Church, they've donned the clothes and vestments of the Catholic Church; they've done their best to convince millions of naïve followers that they actually are the Catholic Church, but they are NOT the Catholic Church and never will be.

The most tragic victims of all this are the children of the duped. They grew up in the counterfeit church, never knowing how evil it is. They were taught by their duped parents and by their duped teachers and "priests" that the Vatican II counterfeit church was the real Catholic Church and they never questioned it.

They had no reason to question it. They trusted their parents and the other adults around them and they believed what they were told. They've since passed those same lies on to their own children, who are now the grandchildren of the duped.

If the first generation to experience these changes in the Church back in the 60s—the so-called "greatest generation" and the first wave of boomers—hadn't been asleep at the wheel, they could have stopped the takeover as it began. At the very least, they could have refused to attend the invalid and non-Catholic New Mass. But they didn't. They did nothing. And now we're left to pick up the pieces.

Some people did resist. Very few, but some. Some priests saw the apostasy taking place and refused to partake in it. Some parents recognized immediately what was happening and passed that knowledge on to their children. We have to give credit to the few.

Your Soul, Your Choice

The first thing most people do when they come across this information is run straight to their parish "priest" who, not surprisingly, calls it all bunk. But guess what? If that "priest" wasn't ordained before 1968, he's not a real priest. How can he be if he wasn't validly ordained? He's a layman who is unwittingly committing mortal sin by posing as a priest.

How can anyone who asks such a person about Vatican II and the invalid New Mass expect to get a truthful answer when the person they're asking doesn't know the truth himself?

Others come across this information, but are leery of priests due to personal experience or because of the massive sex scandals that have erupted within the counterfeit church since Vatican II. They turn to the internet for answers.

That's all well and good, but the majority of websites that call themselves Catholic aren't Catholic at all. They're Vatican II gatekeepers, designed to keep the sheeple within the pen of the counterfeit church. Some of these websites are well-intentioned. Some of them actually believe they are performing a Godly service. They're what Vladimir Lenin called "useful idiots." They unwittingly believe they are working for good, when they are actually working for evil.

In this case, the end result of their actions is exactly the same as the end result of others who possess evil intentions: they convince people that the counterfeit church is Catholic. Thus, despite their good intentions, they contribute to damning souls to hell. They will be held accountable for their sins.

There's no sitting on the fence with this issue. We have to choose individually whether to embrace the true Catholic Faith or follow the herd into the fires of hell. Denial is no longer a valid option, and ignorance is no longer an excuse.

If you want to go to Heaven, you must abandon the millions of duped morons that are on their way to hell and become a traditional Catholic.

What will you choose?

Chapter 7

The Third Secret of Fatima

"Rome will lose the Faith and become the seat of the antichrist." —Our Lady of La Salette, September 19, 1846

In every area of study there are scholars who disagree on various issues. The subject of Fatima is no different. However, there is one aspect of Fatima that every reputable scholar agrees with. They all agree that the Third Secret of Fatima has never been publicly revealed and that it is both a warning and a prophecy from Heaven that the Catholic Church will be infiltrated and subverted, beginning at the very top.

Could they all be right?

Consider the first two secrets of Fatima: a vision of hell and a warning to the world to amend its ways, lest a second, and even deadlier, world war occur. Those are monumental events of enormous importance to the entire human race, both present and future. The Third Secret of Fatima was long rumored to be even more earth-shattering, even more apocalyptic than the first two secrets; its contents so frightening that the Virgin Mary ordered it not to be revealed until the year 1960.

Now look at the explanation put out by the Novus Order church, that the Third Secret of Fatima was a foretelling of the failed assassination attempt on John Paul II. Compare the explosive contents of the first two secrets to the tinny cap-gun pop of the Vatican's interpretation. The Mother of God came down from Heaven to tell us *that?* It's a ludicrous explanation. And no reputable Fatima scholar believes it.

Does it make sense for the Vatican to withhold releasing the Third Secret for 40 years if all it really contained was a message about the wounding of Karol Wojtyla, an event that no one in the entire world, other than those who have been duped into following the Novus Ordo church, could care less about?

Consider also that even among the duped, there were many who couldn't care less. There were wide swaths of liberal Novus Ordo followers who mistook John Paul II to be a conservative and couldn't stand the guy.

Consider the situation in Portugal when the three secrets were first passed on to the children. From the moment the young seers first cast their eyes upon the Mother of God, their lives were plunged into a sea of danger. Remember, between 1910 and 1916, thousands of priests, monks and nuns in Portugal were murdered. The world was also at war. Amidst all that chaos and killing were three children, claiming they saw the Virgin Mary and attracting followers by the thousands, a situation that threatened the very existence of the country's anti-clerical government officials.

The Administrator kidnapped the three children and threatened to boil them in oil. Don't think for a second that the Administrator would not have carried out that threat if he thought he could have gotten away with it. One year after the events of Fatima, a bomb he was making to murder a political opponent exploded in his hands.

Meanwhile, mobs of club-carrying peasants roamed the streets, saying they believed the children, but if the predicted miracle of October 13 did not occur, "they'd better look out for themselves."

On the morning of the miracle, a neighbor of Olimpia Marto, the mother of Francisco and Jacinta, told her, "If the Blessed Virgin doesn't work a miracle today, you and your children will not be alive this evening."

Consider all that and ask yourself if it makes sense for the Virgin Mary to put the three young seers and their families at such grave risk of death if the climatic message of the Third Secret was nothing more than a foretelling of the wounding of a non-Catholic and heretical antipope some sixty years in the future. Of course it doesn't.

On October 13, 1917, three days before the sixth apparition and the Miracle of the Sun, a local Fatima priest,

Father Formigao, questioned Francisco and Jacinta about the Third Secret. They refused to tell him what it was. Father Formigao then asked if the crowd would be sad if they knew the secret. Both children said yes.

Ask yourself, would the crowd, which at the time meant the inhabitants of Fatima and the surrounding villages, be sad about a failed assassination attempt on a non-Catholic and heretical antipope taking place years in the future?

Even if the crowd was duped into believing that John Paul II was a true Catholic Pope, the fact that he survived the attempt on his life would be a cause of joy, not sadness.

In 1946, John M. Haffert, the author of *Meet the Witnesses of the Miracle of the Sun*, spoke with Sister Lucy for four hours. He asked her about the ultimate purpose of the Virgin's visit to Portugal, the ultimate message she wanted to communicate to the world.

Sister Lucy summed up the message in a single sentence: "Men must cease to offend God who is already much offended."

If that is the ultimate message of Fatima, then doesn't it make sense that the Third Secret would correspond to it in some way? And if so, what does Sister Lucy's response have to do with the Vatican's laughable excuse that the Third Secret is a prediction of the failed assassination attempt of a non-Catholic antipope?

It's clear that the Third Secret of Fatima must be something else, something of profound significance;

something much greater than the first two secrets. What could that be?

The Significance of 1960

In 1939, when Sister Lucy first wrote out the Third Secret and placed it in an envelope for her local bishop, she wrote on the outside of the envelope: "Not to be opened until 1960."

In 1946, Sister Lucy told Canon Barthas that the secret was to be revealed in 1960, "Because the Blessed Virgin wishes it so."

In 1955, Cardinal Ottaviani asked Sister Lucy why the Secret was to be revealed in 1960. She told him, "Because it will seem clearer."

In 1957, Sister Lucy told Father Fuentes that the Third Secret would remain a secret until in 1960.

There are numerous other instances of Sister Lucy emphasizing the year 1960 and specifically stating that the Third Secret was to be revealed at that time.

So what was going in the year 1960 that made it so significant to the Third Secret? Was it a plot to assassinate John Paul II some twenty-one years later in 1981? Of course not. Only a fool would believe that.

What was happening in 1960 was the advent of Vatican II and the first in our current line of antipopes, beginning with John XXIII up to and including current antipope Francis.

Remember the significance of January 25? It was on January, 25, 1938 that the unknown light appeared over Europe, as foretold in the Second Secret of Fatima. On that same night, the discussions to begin World War II began during the Christian Rakovsky interrogation.

Fast forward 21 years to 1959, and *on the same day of January 25* antipope John XXIII called for the Vatican II council and the discussions to subvert and destroy the Catholic Church began.

Coincidence?

Reputable Fatima scholars unanimously agree that the Third Secret of Fatima tells of a great apostasy in the Church, beginning at the very top. If they are correct, then such a secret would certainly match and even surpass the significance of the first two secrets. After all, what event could be more catastrophic for mankind than the subversion and attempted destruction of the very Church that God himself established on earth?

If you were to ask most people to describe the most disastrous event that could possibly occur, most would answer a nuclear war that destroys the planet. However, the subversion and takeover of the Catholic Church that we are currently living through is more destructive than nuclear war. In the event of a nuclear war physical lives would be lost. Most would go to hell, but some would be saved. In the current state of the counterfeit church we are in, hundreds of millions of souls are falling by the wayside and going to hell. Such an event doesn't even compare to nuclear war. It is far, far worse.

Nuclear war would destroy lives. The counterfeit church destroys souls. Which is worse?

In the event of nuclear war, many would die instantly. The survivors, seeing the death and destruction, would have time to repent. Like the scoffers who came to Fatima and witnessed the Miracle of the Sun, many would embrace the true Catholic Church and be saved.

The counterfeit church lulls the world to sleep while it engages in a deliberate and coordinated attack to condemn as many souls as possible to the fires of hell. Which is worse?

If the Third Secret of Fatima concerns the subversion of the Church, it would corroborate the statements made by various Vatican insiders, those in position to know.

"Father" Mario Luigi Ciappi, the papal theologian to Pius XII, said about Fatima, "In the Third Secret, it is foretold, among other things, that the great apostasy in the Church will begin at the top."

"Cardinal" Silvio Oddi said, "... the Third Secret ... regards the 'revolution' in the Catholic Church."

The timing of 1960 would also make sense. If the Third Secret foretells the current apostasy in the Church, and if Catholics around the world had been alerted to that fact in 1960, they could have resisted en masse and prevented it.

In fact, if the Third Secret of Fatima is a warning of the current apostasy taking place in the Church, then everything suddenly fits and makes sense: the timing of the year 1960, the significance of the message, the statements made by Vatican insiders, everything.

The Vatican's claim that the Third Secret is about the attempted assassination attempt of John Paul II is so laughably bad it would be funny if it weren't so tragic.

It's All About Him

Have you ever known someone who only wanted to talk about themselves? You could be telling them about the horrible traffic accident you just witnessed, with broken glass and dead bodies all over the street, and they'd change the subject to the fender bender they had last summer.

You could be telling them about the new car you just bought and within seconds they'd be telling you about the new car *they* just bought.

You could be telling them about the big raise or the big promotion you just received and before you knew it, they'd be telling you about *their* big raise or *their* big promotion.

Meet John Paul II.

The Mother of God gave us the Rosary. John Paul II tried to make the Rosary all about him with his own set of mysteries.

The Mother of God gave us Fatima, the Miracle of the Sun, and the Third Secret. John Paul II tried to make those events all about him by claiming that the Third Secret foretold the failed assassination attempt on his life.

God gave us the world and everything living on it. John Paul II tried to make the world all about him by having the impostor Sister Lucy claim at her 1992-93 interviews that his consecration of Russia in 1984 was responsible for stopping a nuclear war with the Soviets in 1985.

John Paul II tried to usurp the Rosary by making it all about him. He tried to usurp the Third Secret of Fatima by making it all about him. And he tried to usurp God by making himself the savior of the world. Has a more narcissistic individual ever walked the face of the earth? With the imposter Sister Lucy's preposterous claim that he singlehandedly saved the world from nuclear destruction, it's as if John Paul II tried to make himself God.

Joseph Stalin and Vladimir Lenin tortured and murdered millions of people, but they didn't purposely deceive them in order to condemn them to hell.

John Paul II, along with the other antipopes of the Vatican II counterfeit church, duped millions of people into accepting the non-Catholic and invalid New Mass, thereby condemning their souls to hell. Isn't that more evil than anything Stalin or Lenin ever did?

There are pictures of John Paul II available online showing him engaged in Masonic handshakes, along with pictures of him throwing up the 666 sign and holding it over his eye, signifying the eye of Horus. In fact, there are pictures of him doing just that on the back cover of this book.

Making the 666 sign or the eye of Horus sign is signaling to the world that one is a Freemason aka a Satanist with a burning hatred for Jesus Christ. Anyone who denies that is an imbecile with no knowledge of those symbols or what they represent.

Albert Pike, the supreme head of Freemasonry, described who Freemasons worship in his book *Morals and Dogma*:

> "Lucifer the Light-Bearer! Strange and mysterious name to give to the Spirit of Darkness! Lucifer, the Son of the Morning! Is it he who bears the Light, and with its splendors intolerable blinds feeble, sensual, or selfish souls? Doubt it not!"

Eliphas Levi, another high-ranking Freemason, said the exact same thing in his book *The History of Magic*. Levi was Pike's mentor.

William T. Still writes in his book *The New World Order: The Ancient Plan of Secret Societies*:

> "Though few Masons know it, the god of Masonry is Lucifer."

A. Ralph Epperson writes in his book *The New World Order*:

"The Masons know that they must conceal their horrible secret from the people. That secret is simply the fact that certain of their members worship Lucifer."

William Schnoebelen writes in his book *Masonry Beyond the Light:*

"Set (Lucifer) is the acknowledged god of Masonry."

The well-known New Age philosopher David Spangler was a board member of the Planetary Initiative for the World We Choose, an organization of the Economic and Social Council of the United Nations.

Here's what he wrote on pages 43-45 of his book *Reflections on the Christ*:

"... the light that reveals us the path to the Christ comes from Lucifer. He is the light giver. He is aptly named the Morning Star because it is his light that heralds for man the dawn of a greater consciousness.

"Lucifer works within each of us to bring us to wholeness, and as we move into a new age, which is the age of man's wholeness, each of us in some way is brought to that point which I term the Luciferic initiation, the particular doorway through which the individual must pass if he is to come fully into the presence of his light and his wholeness.

"Lucifer comes to give to us the final gift of wholeness. If we accept it then he is free and we are free. That is the Luciferic initiation. It is one that many people now, and in the days ahead, will be facing, for it is an initiation into the New Age."

Are you convinced yet? Every 33rd degree Freemason is taught that Lucifer is their God.

The Church, in its study of secret societies, wrote the following about Freemasonry in the Acta Sancta Sedis in 1865:

"If one takes into consideration the immense development which these secret societies have attained, the length of time they are persevering in their vigor; their furious aggressiveness; the tenacity with which their members cling to the association and to the false principals it professes; the persevering mutual cooperation of so many different types of men in the promotion of evil; one can hardly deny that the supreme architect of these associations (seeing that the cause must be proportional to the effect) can be none other than he who in the sacred writings is styled the prince of the world; and that Satan himself even by his physical cooperation, directs and inspires at least the leaders of these bodies, physically cooperating with them."

You can make the claim, a pretty lame one, that John Paul II was only joking when he made those 666 and eye of Horus signs, but why would a real pope do that? What kind of a joke is it for a so-called pope to signal allegiance to a religious cult that worships Satan? And how about all of those Masonic handshakes he is photographed making?

Don't believe me? Look up the pictures yourself. There are plenty of pictures online for you to research that show *all* of the antipopes from the late 1950s on, including current antipope Francis, making the 666 sign, making the devil horns sign, making the hidden hand sign of Freemasonry (putting the hand inside one's shirt or coat, like Napoleon), engaging in Masonic handshakes, etc. You name it; they're doing it without exception. Photo after photo after photo.

Can you imagine any of the real popes of the past doing such things?

And did I mention that the Grand Orient Lodge of Italian Freemasonry awarded John Paul II their greatest honor, the Order of Galilee, for promoting Freemasonic ideals?

Emil Mazey: "I can't prove you are a Communist. But when I see a bird that quacks like a duck, walks like a duck, has feathers and webbed feet and associates with ducks—I'm certainly going to assume that he is a duck."

Me: "I can't prove you are a Freemason and therefore a Satanist. But when I see a man who talks like a Freemason, shakes hands like a Freemason, makes Freemasonic signs with his fingers and associates with known Freemasons—I'm certainly going to assume that he is a Freemason."

Impostor deniers: "I can't prove you are a Freemason and therefore a Satanist. But when I see a man who talks like a Freemason, shakes hands like a Freemason, makes Freemasonic signs with his fingers and associates with known Freemasons—then because I'm too brainwashed to think for myself, I'm certainly going to assume that he is not a Freemason."

Chapter 8

The Consecration of Russia ... Did it Really Happen?

In the previous chapter we discussed the unanimous agreement of reputable Fatima scholars concerning the Third Secret. One aspect of Fatima that has no such agreement is the issue of the Consecration of Russia. Some say it took place, others say it didn't. Still others argue over the date of when it allegedly took place. What's the truth? Did the consecration of Russia actually take place, and if so, when?

The answer, which may shock you, is yes, it took place.

The Consecration of Russia took place on July 7, 1952. On that date, Pope Pious XII specifically consecrated Russia to the Immaculate Heart of Mary. That is a fact that no one can deny.

You can read about the pope's consecration of Russia on page 507 of the book *The Truth about What Really Happened to the Catholic Church after Vatican II* by Brother Michael Dimond and Brother Peter Dimond.

You can also read the exact words of Pope Pius XII right here in his Apostolic Letter, Sacro Vergente Anno, dated July 7, 1952:

"And we, so that our fervent prayers and yours may more easily be heard, and to give you a special testimony of our particular benevolence, just as a few years ago we consecrated the entire human race to the Immaculate Heart of the Virgin Mary, Mother of God, so today we consecrate and in a most special manner we entrust all the peoples of Russia to this Immaculate Heart, with the firm hope that soon, thanks to the all-powerful patronage of the Blessed Virgin Mary, the wishes which we form with all of you and all good men may be happily fulfilled, for a true peace, fraternal concord and the liberty due to all, and in the first place to the Church. Thus by our prayer, united to your own and that of the whole Christian people, the Kingdom of the Savior Jesus Christ will be firmly established over all the earth: A Kingdom of truth and life, a Kingdom of holiness and grace, a Kingdom of justice, love and peace."

So there it is, in black and white; clear proof which no one can dispute. The Consecration of Russia did indeed take place. Anyone who tells you otherwise is either misinformed, a liar, or both.

As a result of Pius XII's Consecration of Russia in July of 1952, the Korean War, which had been raging since 1950, slowed down and ended a year later.

There was Communist violence and bloodshed in Vietnam, in Cambodia and elsewhere, but the predominantly Christian countries of Europe and the United States were spared, and the U.S. became a refuge for those who managed to escape Communist regimes. The Cuban Missile Crisis, which threatened to plunge the world into nuclear war, deescalated quickly. The Berlin Wall came down.

This was the "certain period of peace" promised by Our Lady and it all occurred decades ago. Those who expected then or who continue to expect today a period of continual peace and bliss are misguided. We were never promised anything more than a temporary reprieve and that was conditional on both the Consecration of Russia and the avoidance of sin. The Consecration was done, but our country's sinful ways have not abated. They've increased.

A nation that condones the sin of abortion, the sin of homosexual union and marriage, the sin of pornography, the sin of immodest dress and others cannot expect to remain at peace. Such an expectation is impossible given that a country that not only allows but also promotes such sins is in direct violation of God's laws. A country like that cannot expect to remain untouched by God's wrath and so Communism has reared its ugly head once again with the Communist subversion of our own government.

The Conversion of Russia

While we're on the subject of the Consecration of Russia, let's tackle another common Fatima misconception, the conversion of Russia. In speaking to the children at the third apparition on July 13, 1917, Our Lady said, "In the end my Immaculate Heart will triumph. The Holy Father will consecrate Russia to me, and it will be converted and a certain period of peace will be granted to the world."

Many people think that Our Lady's words about Russia, "and it will be converted," mean a conversion to Catholicism, but that's not the case at all and it can be easily proven.

First, throughout the six Fatima apparitions, as well as other reported apparitions, the Blessed Virgin has always been very precise in her speech. She doesn't say anything ambiguous or confusing. In this case, she specifically said "and it will be converted," but she made no mention of religious conversion. She didn't say "it will be converted to Catholicism" or "it will be converted to Christianity," she only said "it will be converted."

The definition of the word "convert" is "to change in form, character or function." Isn't that exactly what happened in Russia after Pius XII consecrated the country to Mary's Immaculate Heart? The persecution and murder of tens of millions of Christians ceased.

Second, and almost everyone seems to forget this, Our Lady used a form of the word "convert" several other times in the Fatima apparitions. At the second apparition on June 13, 1917, Lucy asked for a sick person to be healed. Our Lady responded, "If he is converted he will be cured during the year." Note that once again there is no mention made of converting to the Catholic Faith.

On page 112 of the book *Miracles* by Jean Helle, the author says that the sick person in question was someone that a neighbor of Lucy's mother had recommended. That right there tells us that the sick person was most likely already a Catholic. We know this for several reasons.

One, the neighbor who requested help for the sick man must have been Catholic or she would not have appealed for help from the Blessed Virgin. A non-Catholic person would never ask the Blessed Virgin for help.

Two, if the sick man was a friend of the neighbor, then he was most likely a local resident; otherwise how would he know the neighbor? Remember this was in 1917. Lucy's neighbors didn't have cars, telephones, or contrary to what some people reading this might think, the internet. There were no bus or train stations nearby. People rarely strayed more than a few miles from their homes. They had no desire to, and even if they did, they were too busy working and raising families to do so. So where and how did Lucy's neighbor meet the sick man? He must have been a local resident, which means he was almost certainly a Catholic.

Despite the revolution of 1910, Portugal was a predominantly Catholic country. According to the book *Our Lady of Light* by Chanoine Barthas and Pere G. Da Fonesca, the hamlet of Aljustrel where Lucy lived consisted of only twelve small houses in 1917. In her memoirs, Lucy writes about the neighborhood children coming to stay at her house and how those children were present when Lucy's mother gave catechism lessons. Lucy also writes in her memoirs about the neighborhood children going to communion, and about the dances and the courtship of the young people and the weddings of her older sisters.

That tells us that the entire hamlet and most likely the surrounding hamlets were all Catholic. After all, the parents of the children wouldn't allow them to be present for catechism lessons if they weren't Catholic, and the parents of the young people wouldn't allow their sons and daughters to be mingling at dances with non-Catholics or to marry non-Catholics. The weddings might not even be valid. This was a small, close knit hamlet of Catholic families, and the surrounding hamlets were undoubtedly the same.

Taking all of the above into consideration, the evidence overwhelmingly points to the sick man already being Catholic. So when the Blessed Mother said, "If he is converted he will be cured during the year," what the word "converted" meant wasn't converted to the Catholic faith, because he was already Catholic. It meant a change in his sinful ways. In other words, if he is converted, if he changes his life, stops sinning and amends his ways, he would be cured. Doesn't it make sense now?

Our Lady also used a version of the word "convert" when she said, "Do you wish to offer yourselves to God, to endure all the suffering that He may please to send you, as an act of reparation for the sins by which He is offended, and to ask for the conversion of sinners?"

Once again, Our Lady does not specifically ask that sinners be converted to Catholicism, only that they be converted, which could also mean changed. If you assume that Our Lady *does* mean the conversion of sinners to the Catholic Faith, then all the sacrifices she asked the children to make would only be for non-Catholics. Because what would be the point to make sacrifices so someone who is already Catholic would convert to Catholicism?

Does it make sense to you that the Mother of God would come down from Heaven and ask only for sacrifices to convert non-Catholics to the Catholic Faith, but say nothing about making sacrifices for the sins of people who are already Catholic? Catholics sin too, and if nobody is praying for them, they can also go to hell.

On the other hand, if the word "conversion" meant change, then it makes sense, because Catholics are no longer excluded. To ask for the conversion of sinners now means both the conversion to the Catholic Faith for non-Catholics *and* a call to change, to quit sinning, for those who are already Catholic.

Going back to Our Lady's use of precise speech, it's logical that she would intend the same meaning for a word each time she used it. To do otherwise would only lead to confusion. When talking about the sick man converting in order to be cured or of making sacrifices for the conversion of sinners, her words only make sense if the intention is a change of life, from sinning to non-sinning.

Therefore, it is only logical that the same meaning is behind Our Lady's words regarding Russia. To assume otherwise indicates imprecise and confusing speech on the part of Our Lady.

Sister Lucy also uses the word "convert" several times in her memoirs. In each instance, it makes sense if the word is intended to mean change. She writes of the poor thief who danced with Jacinta in the jail:

"We only hope that Our Lady has had pity on his soul and converted him."

There is no mention of the thief becoming Catholic; only that he change from a sinner to a non-sinner.

Don't be fooled by those who erroneously insist that Our Lady intended for the entire country of Russia to convert to the Catholic Faith. She obviously meant a change from their murderous ways to a more peaceful country.

Chapter 9

Why So Many Refuse to Believe

"How easy it is to make people believe a lie, and how hard it is to undo that work again." —Mark Twain

Human beings are a dichotomy. On the one hand, they're geniuses, capable of inventing the computer, the automobile, air conditioning and the telephone. On the other hand, they're gullible dolts, easily duped and swayed by smooth-talking hustlers and authority figures.

How do we account for those who are willfully blind? How do we explain the mental manipulation of those who obstinately insist that Sister Lucy and her impostor are one and the same person? How do we excuse the actions of those who sinfully pledge their allegiance to a corrupt, non-Catholic counterfeit church and its unbroken succession of antipopes? Just what is going on with these people?

Stupidity plays a part, obviously, but even more than stupidity is fear.

You may have heard from people who study such things that man's greatest fear is public speaking, but it actually goes much deeper than that. Man's greatest fear is non-conformity.

People are frightened of being different, of standing out, of not fitting in. That's why they all dress the same, think the same, and act the same. Being different is terrifying. It's a fear so prevalent and so intense that faced with a choice between embracing a lie in order to fit in with the herd, or accepting the truth and standing out as someone different, most people will embrace the lie.

If you find it difficult to believe that millions of people can be so easily duped, so easily frightened this way, take a look at all the dopes running around today wearing face masks. Only about five percent of them actually believe the masks work. The remaining majority, well over 90%, aren't convinced the masks work, but they're wearing them anyway because of peer pressure, because they're afraid to stand out; afraid to be different. That can be easily proved by looking at places that have lifted their mask mandates.

Look at Florida and Texas and what do you see? You see that 90% of the people that *were* wearing masks for the last twelve months aren't wearing them now. Some still are, around 5%. Those are the people who truly believe the mask offers them protection. They believed it before and they believe it now. You have to give them credit for their conviction, if nothing else.

But the vast majority of people have stopped wearing masks and the reason why they've stopped is because now it's socially acceptable not to wear one. If they actually believed the masks worked they would keep them on. After all, if their masks worked for the last twelve months, they should still be working now.

When the herd was wearing masks, they wore masks, because they wanted to fit in. Now that the herd is not wearing masks, they're not, again because they want to fit in. If the herd went back to wearing masks tomorrow, so would they. *Everything they believe, everything they do, is dictated by the herd.* And they represent the vast majority of the human race.

Purple Dunce Caps

I'll go you one better. Suppose tomorrow you turned on your television and saw every newscaster on every news station wearing a purple dunce cap. Suppose you continued to watch and saw that every one of these dunce-cap-wearing newscasters was shilling hard for *you* to wear a purple dunce cap, claiming it would save your life.

Suppose medical "experts" appeared on these same newscasts, also wearing purple dunce caps and also shilling hard for you to wear a purple dunce cap by claiming it would save your life.

Suppose these newscasts began airing nonstop, doctored footage of people falling ill and dying because they weren't wearing purple dunce caps.

Suppose your family members and friends began wearing purple dunce caps and urged you to do the same.

Suppose you looked out your window and saw people walking down the street while wearing purple dunce caps, driving their cars while wearing purple dunce caps, and going to work while wearing purple dunce caps.

Suppose businesses began posting signs on their doors demanding that all of their customers wear purple dunce caps.

I guarantee you—I absolute, double-down guarantee you—that every single person you see wearing a face mask today, would be wearing a purple dunce cap tomorrow.

That's human behavior in a nutshell and the people reading this who are now offended would be the very first ones to don a purple dunce cap.

How do I know all this? I'm not a mind-reader, but I am a student of human nature. I'm also a traditional Catholic and once you embrace the true Catholic Faith it's like having X-ray vision into what people are thinking and why they behave the way they do. It's impossible to lie to a traditional Catholic, so don't ever try. They'll see through you every time.

What I've just described with the purple dunce caps is exactly how human beings behave and that behavior is nothing new. It's no different than the old Hans Christian Andersen story *The Emperor Wears No Clothes.*

Andersen was describing the people of his time in 1837, and they're exactly like the people of our time. In fact, Anderson's story was based on an earlier version written in 1335, so that tells you how human behavior is timeless.

I don't think Andersen would be the least bit surprised if he knew how his story has played out in reality in our current time. He was a student of human behavior too.

In times past, to be different from the herd meant more than just ridicule, it meant the risk of ostracism. People lived in small communities and villages, and anyone who dared to be different was at risk of being thrown out. Back then, being thrown out often led to starvation and death. That's the underlying motive behind the fear of being different.

Those who dare to be different today are no longer thrown out of villages, but they are ostracized in other ways. Their books are banned and their businesses are boycotted. They're cancelled on social media, abandoned by so-called friends, and even arrested.

People today and throughout all of history are such spineless cowards they will abandon their so-called values and principles, which they have loudly bragged about all their life, in order to avoid the slightest risk of ostracism.

This kind of social pressure is so strong it causes people to believe lies, or to at least claim they believe lies, which is a lie in itself. Numerous studies have been conducted along those lines and the results are always the same. For every courageous individual who insists on telling the truth, regardless of social pressure, there are dozens of frightened simpletons who publicly discount what their own eyes have shown them to be true. So they lie in order to fit in. They know they're lying, but they do it anyway.

People also have an emotional stake in their opinions and false beliefs, and they become frightened when those opinions and beliefs are exposed as lies. It's often less a case of not believing than of not *wanting* to believe.

In regards to the issue of an impostor Sister Lucy and the infiltration and subversion of the Catholic Church, people have written books in praise of the Vatican II counterfeit church. Some of them have websites and blogs in praise of the Vatican II counterfeit church. They've raised their families to believe in the legitimacy of the Vatican II counterfeit church. They're friends with the "priests" of the Vatican II counterfeit church and they participate in the non-Catholic and invalid New Mass. Their social life and the education of their children revolves around the Vatican II counterfeit church.

That's a lot to renounce, a lot to give up. It takes a strong person—a very strong person—to say, "I was wrong. The bastards lied to me."

Most people don't have that level of honesty or courage. They need to be told what to think and how to live their lives. If you point out to them that their fear is leading them to hell, it makes no difference. In their minds, it's better to hide from reality and end up in hell rather than to admit they were wrong and face the fear of ostracism.

To acknowledge that they've been duped in any area of life is not only an affront to their pride it also forces them to question whether they've been duped in other areas of life. It forces them to question an entire lifetime of accumulated opinions and beliefs; forces them to wonder whether everything they've ever been taught or told isn't also a lie. For most people, that is positively frightening.

So they take the easy way out. They bury their head in the sand and pretend to believe what they know are lies. Over time, they come to actually believe the lies.

They never attempt to refute the evidence. It can't be refuted. So they either ignore it or renounce it without study. That is the sad state of the majority of the human race.

The brainwashing is so complete, so all-encompassing, that the masses do not even realize it's occurring. Their opinions and thoughts are put into their head by others, their behavior and actions are planned and manipulated by others, yet they have no clue.

Ask them about it and they'll deny it. Press them on it and they'll become angry. Yet the truth is undeniable. They're being led around by their nose from birth to death and they don't even know it.

Harboring Secret Sins

So we have stupidity and we have fear as major reasons why so many people choose the path of the willfully blind. But there's also a third reason and it might be the most important one of all. In my experience, those who choose to remain willfully blind, do so because they are harboring secret sins. By choosing to remain blind to the truth they are able to cling to their sins.

Take someone who is married and practicing the mortal sin of birth control or Natural Family Planning. By denying the truth of an impostor Sister Lucy and an apostate counterfeit church, truth that their own eyes can readily see, they are able to cling to their sins without feeling any remorse.

Take someone who is committing the mortal sin of attending the non-Catholic and invalid New Mass. By denying the truth of an impostor Sister Lucy and an apostate counterfeit church, they are able to reap the benefits of social interaction with others who also choose to remain willfully blind without feeling any remorse.

Take a "priest" or "bishop" of the Vatican II counterfeit church. By denying the truth of an impostor Sister Lucy and an apostate counterfeit church, they are able to reap the benefits of continual employment and prestige without feeling any remorse.

Do you see how deep this can go?

How about the woman who refuses to dress modestly, because she likes the attention she receives? She can only justify it by denying the existence of an impostor Sister Lucy and an apostate counterfeit church.

How about the union man who votes for pro-abort politicians, knowing full well how sinful they are, but doing it anyway because he knows they are pro-union and will help put more money in his pocket? He justifies his actions by pointing out that the "bishops" of the counterfeit church endorse the candidate. In order to fool himself in this way he has to deny the existence of an impostor Sister Lucy and an apostate counterfeit church. (As you know, to vote for a pro-abort politician, which includes most Republicans and virtually all Democrats, is a mortal sin that will send such a person straight to hell if not confessed to a validly ordained priest.)

Take a close look at the people in your own life who choose to remain willfully blind and you'll see that each and every one of them is harboring a secret sin; a sin that their denial of the truth allows them to continue without remorse. You'll also find that the more insistent they are at denying the truth, the deeper their sins go.

This is all backed up by the Bible. Thessalonians 2:10 tells us:

"And in all seduction of iniquity to them that perish: because they receive not the love of the truth, that they might be saved. Therefore God shall send them the operation of error, to believe lying: That all may be judged who have not believed the truth but have consented to iniquity."

Heaven or Hell?

If you were to ask the average person on the street if they would rather go to Heaven or hell, they will tell you Heaven, obviously. And yet their actions say the exact opposite.

Non-Catholics continue to show no interest in converting to the true Catholic faith, while those who claim to be Catholic continue to commit mortal sin by attending the non-Catholic and invalid New Mass.

Just as there are RINOS (Republicans in Name Only), there are CINOS (Catholics in Name Only). They call themselves Catholic, but they attend the non-Catholic and invalid New Mass. They call themselves Catholic, but they vote for pro-abort politicians. They call themselves Catholic, but they support open borders, rioting in the streets, and looting. They call themselves Catholic, but they continue to dress immodestly, read and watch pornography, and practice birth control. In other words, they call themselves Catholic, but their actions are decidedly non-Catholic. They call themselves Catholic, but they continue to commit one mortal sin after another. They're all going to hell.

How do you deal with such stupidity, with such fear, with such refusal to face reality and such stubbornness in clinging to sin? I'll be the first to tell you, it's not easy. If someone is flat-out determined to ignore the truth and condemn their soul to hell, then there's really very little that can be done to save them.

If you spend too much time trying to save someone who doesn't want to be saved, you end up putting your own soul at risk. Remember, misery loves company. There's nothing a miserable sinner likes more than dragging other miserable sinners down to hell with them. So be careful. Don't let them influence or sway you with their own false beliefs. They could catch you off guard in a down moment and fill your head with doubts; convince you that sin is good and "look at all the fun you're missing. See that blond over there? She likes you and I have her number. I can set you up." Then the next thing you know, your soul is swirling in a downward spiral of mortal sin. *Don't take that risk.* Remain uncompromising and don't continue to spend time with people who choose to remain blind.

The best you can do with such people is plant a seed and hope it takes root. Most likely, it won't, but you never know. Present them with a book, a video, an article, whatever you have. Strike up a conversation. Do what you can. But don't be surprised that so many of them choose hell over Heaven. You're dealing with people who are too timid to think for themselves; too frightened to differ from the herd; too brainwashed to recognize and acknowledge reality when it's right in front of their face.

The downside to that approach is time. We're literally living in the end times. Time is short and growing shorter by the day.

The sad truth is very few people make it to Heaven, and that includes Catholics. Nobody outside of the Catholic Church makes it to Heaven, and very few people who claim to be Catholic make it to Heaven. That leaves only a miniscule number of people. Out of the next fifty thousand people you pass on the street, maybe one of them will make it to Heaven, the rest will not.

That's a sobering thought. It means almost all of your family, friends, co-workers and associates are going to burn in hell for all eternity.

Do what you can. Plant that seed. And work out your own salvation with fear and trembling

"And he said to him: If they hear not Moses and the prophets, neither will they believe if one rise again from the dead." —Luke 16:31

Chapter 10

Fatima's Relevance for Today

Suppose you were convicted of a crime, a crime so serious that the judge, if he wanted to, could sentence you to death. And suppose the mother of the judge came to your cell on the night before your sentencing and offered to use her influence with her son to spare your life; to get all of the charges against you dropped and have her son issue you a pardon.

But instead of accepting this offer from the mother of the judge, you snubbed her and refused to talk to her. Or worse, you insulted her and told all of the other prisoners to insult her too.

Do you think that would be a smart way to behave? What kind of a sentence do you think the judge is going to give you when he hears how you ignored and insulted his mother?

This is the lesson of Fatima.

The judge is Jesus Christ.

His mother is the Blessed Virgin.

We are all waiting to be sentenced.

111

The Holy Mother is offering us, all of humanity, one last opportunity to change our ways, lest we be punished here on earth by wars and persecution, and punished even worse in the afterlife by an eternity burning in the fires of hell. To save our lives here on earth, and more importantly, to save our souls in the afterlife, the Blessed Virgin implores us to stop sinning, to say the Rosary, and to make sacrifices for the love of Jesus, for sinners, and in reparation for sins against her Immaculate Heart.

A person can choose to ignore these pleadings of the Blessed Virgin. They can insult the Blessed Virgin, just like they can insult the mother of the judge. But I wouldn't want to be in their place when they try to explain their behavior to the ultimate judge.

The Blessed Virgin also gave us the Third Secret of Fatima with explicit instructions that it be released in the year 1960 or at the time of Sister Lucy's death, whichever came first. Reputable Fatima scholars unanimously agree that the Third Secret of Fatima foretold of a massive infiltration and subversion of the Catholic Church, beginning at the very top. Those entrusted with the Third Secret have chosen to hide its true message and to release instead a fabricated version of it in order to deceive humanity. Those who have done this claim to be Catholic, but are not. They have created a counterfeit church and a non-Catholic and invalid New Mass that is a mortal sin to attend. Barring a last minute conversion, they are all going to hell when they die and they want to take as many souls as they can to hell with them. They want to take you to hell.

The question now is what do you intend to do about it? Do you have the courage and desire to know the truth? Or are you a coward, too frightened to acknowledge what your own eyes are telling you, and too brainwashed to break free from your programming?

"If you say the Rosary faithfully until death, I do assure you that, in spite of the gravity of your sins, you shall receive a never fading crown of glory. Even if you are on the brink of damnation, even if you have one foot in Hell, even if you have sold your soul to the devil as sorcerers do who practice black magic, and even if you are a heretic as obstinate as a devil, sooner or later you will be converted and amend your life and save your soul, if—and mark well what I say—if you say the Holy Rosary devoutly every day until death for the purpose of knowing the truth and obtaining contrition and pardon for your sins." —St. Louis De Montfort, *The Secret of the Rosary*

Chapter 11

Fatima's Relevance to You

In order to be saved, in order to go to Heaven, you must become a traditional Catholic.

I can hear the groans and howls of indignation right now from some readers. I can hear the whiny complaints that the Catholic Church is not Biblical. The reality is the exact opposite. The Catholic Church is entirely Biblical. In fact, it's the only religion in the world whose teachings are confirmed in the Bible.

Penance, purgatory, confession, Holy Communion—it's all in the Bible, including the Hail Mary prayer (Luke 1:28 and 1:42) and the Immaculate Heart of Mary (Luke 2:35). Don't believe me? Read the book *The Bible Proves the Teachings of the Catholic Church* by Brother Peter Dimond and see for yourself. That is, if you have the courage to do so.

If you don't already know that everything the Catholic Church teaches is confirmed in the Bible, then it means you've been misled. There's no shame in that. We've all been misled. The shame lies in being too stubborn or too stupid to admit it. Now is the time to discover for yourself the true Church of Jesus Christ.

If it's Heaven you seek, don't discount the only religion in the world with a history of documented miracles. From the Shroud of Turin (the burial cloth of Jesus Christ) to the tilma of Guadalupe (a supernatural imprint of the Mother of God); from the Miracle of the Sun at Fatima to the uncorrupt bodies of saints and seers (bodies which refuse to decay after death), the Catholic Church has it all. No other religion has a single documented miracle to its name; the Catholic Church has thousands.

If it's God's love you desire, consider carefully a religion whose churches, hospitals, schools and missions have done more good for more people than any other organization in the history of the world.

Don't be in a rush to dismiss a religion that has saved Christianity and the entire world from destruction countless times, most notably in the Battle of Lepanto on October 7, 1571.

If not for the courageous men and women of the Catholic Church and the Popes who led them, the entire world today would be speaking Arabic and practicing Islam. You, yourself, would never have been born if not for the strength and bravery of past Catholics.

The plain truth is that membership in the Catholic Church is absolutely necessary for salvation, but-that means belonging to the *true* Catholic Church, not the wicked, non-Catholic counterfeit church that calls itself Catholic.

Protestants and other non-Catholics have been greatly misled about the true Catholic Church. They hear about the sex scandals, the Freemasonic antipopes, and the apostasy coming from Rome and rightly conclude that those behind it and those who support it are wicked and evil. And they're right. Those behind it and those who support it *are* wicked and evil, but they have nothing to do with the true Catholic Church.

The post Vatican II counterfeit church is wicked indeed, no one denies that. It's the *pre* Vatican II Catholic Church, the *true* Catholic Church that's necessary for salvation. Without it, you will be damned to hell for all eternity.

There are three steps to becoming a traditional Catholic. First, you must believe in the teachings of the true Catholic Church. Second, you must be baptized Catholic. Third, you must live the remainder of your life as a traditional Catholic. That includes never attending a non-Catholic service, such as the New Mass, ever again, and going to confession with a validly ordained Catholic priest (a priest ordained before 1968). The steps to do all of these things are available at the following two websites www.MostHolyFamilyMonastery.com and www.VaticanCatholic.com.

What else is required? You will have to detach from the world; to be in the world, but not of the world. You must also pray the Rosary and you must stop sinning.

Sins of the Flesh

Lust, sodomy, sex outside of marriage, immodest dress, pornography, self-abuse, divorce and remarriage ... these are the "sins of the flesh" that little Jacinta warned us about; the sins that condemn more souls to hell than any other.

Of course, Jacinta didn't specify these exact sins; she was only nine-years-old when she died. But she did tell us that the Holy Mother confided in her that more people go to hell for sins of the flesh than for any other reason.

You could make a case that when the Blessed Virgin communicated that information to Jacinta she was speaking strictly about Catholics. That's because the actual reason why most people go to hell is because they are outside the Catholic Church. Then again, perhaps Our Lady was speaking for all people with the understanding that the reason why most people don't become Catholic is because they want to continue dressing immodestly, continue having sex outside of marriage, continue having access to abortion and divorce. In other words, sins of the flesh. That certainly seems to be the reason why most Protestants won't become Catholic. Like Henry VIII, they're driven by lust. They're also terrified of confession.

Almost everyone on earth today is engaged in sins of the flesh and therefore on a fast-track to hell.

If sins of the flesh are indeed the primary reason why most people are condemned to hell, you can increase your chances of going to Heaven tremendously by eliminating those sins from your life.

Stop Digging

If you've dug yourself into a hole of mortal sin, the first thing to do is stop digging. In other words, stop sinning. Stop it immediately. Easier said than done, I admit, but do you want to go to Heaven when you die, or do you want to burn in the fires of hell? Obviously, you want to go to Heaven or you would not be reading this book.

Other than within a committed marriage, wouldn't it be easier to just lay off the sex? Meaningless sex is just that, meaningless, and it will send you straight to hell. Don't you sometimes (all the time) feel worse afterwards due to guilt and shame? And isn't pornography a hundred times worse? Why not clean up your act?

I can't speak for women, but for men the act of sex is as much about the girl's acceptance as it is about the physical release. The girl's acceptance is like a pat on the head, which is pretty pathetic when you think about it. But if feeds the ego and most men have fragile egos.

Have you ever noticed how the world's biggest pickup artists, the men most in need of constant sex, have the most fragile egos of all? They're walking bundles of insecurity, continuously seeking female approval. You don't need that. The only person whose approval you should seek is God's.

Have your sins become an addiction? The best way to cure an addiction is to quit cold turkey. And one of the keys to going cold turkey is avoiding the people, places and things that lead to sin.

You've heard the expression out of sight, out of mind. There's a lot of wisdom to those words. Put them to use by cleansing your computer of any images or content that might tempt you to sin, and by ridding your home of every movie, book, magazine, and article of clothing that could possibly lead you to sin or tempt someone else to sin. Purge it all from your life.

Every time you flee from the occasion of sin, it's a crown of glory earned for you in Heaven. Every wicked invitation you turn down is a feather in your cap before God. Every sinful person you release from your life, including those nice, pleasant-to-be-around family members and friends, earns you another song from the Heavenly choir of angels.

So what *can* you do as a Catholic? The answer is not much. Get ready for a boring life, but only in terms of living in the world. You won't be missing much.

Everything on television and at the movies today is trash, and that won't be changing anytime soon, if ever.

Streaming services are even worse. Any parent that allows their children to watch television of any sort is putting both their soul and the souls of their children at risk of eternal damnation.

Video games I'm not familiar with, but I suspect they're trash too.

Professional sports are a woke joke.

With the rare exception of a handful of independent authors, all fiction and most non-fiction being published today and for the last several decades is trash.

Music is Satanic. I'm not kidding. Aside from most classical music, everything being made today, whether rock, pop, rap, metal, country, easy listening, you name it is literally Satanic.

Rid your life of all of the above. Just dump it, get rid of it. It can only cause harm to your soul.

That doesn't leave a whole lot.

You'll have to find your fun elsewhere, in the laughter of children and the beauty of nature; in solitude and quiet contemplation. Find your peace in prayer and your joy in a playful pet.

Look at all the time you'll have to pray, to think about God, to make restitution to those you need to make restitution to.

You can exercise. If you have kids you can help them build models, solve puzzles and play board games like Scrabble.

You may have to remove people from your life. In fact, I guarantee you'll have to do that. Friends, family members, acquaintances, co-workers ... if they're not for God, cut them loose. That means almost everyone in your life has to go.

Withdraw from the world and embrace solitude. Become your own best friend if you're not already.

If you think you have it tough by giving up a handful of vain pleasures, look at what the Apostles suffered:

Saint Matthew was beheaded in Egypt.

Saint Andrew was crucified in Greece.

Saint Philip was crucified in Asia, Minor.

Saint Bartholomew (Nathaniel) was skinned alive and crucified.

Saint Paul was beheaded.

Saint Peter was crucified upside down.

Saint Matthias (chosen to replace Judas) was burned alive.

Saint Thomas was pierced to death.

Saint Mark was dragged to death.

Saint Simon was sawn in half.

Saint Jude was crucified.

Saint James, son of Alpheus, was stoned and clubbed to death.

Saint James, son of Zebedee, was beheaded.

Saint Stephen was stoned to death.

And you're complaining because you can't watch television.

Is Heaven Fun?

I'll be honest with you, being a Catholic is hard. The hardest path you'll ever follow in your life. It's definitely not for the weak or cowardly, and if your goal in life is having fun, you won't like being Catholic.

But what's your alternative, burning in the fires of hell for all eternity? That doesn't sound like much fun either.

At none of the Fatima apparitions did Our Lady appear to be having fun. The children described her as always looking serious, never smiling or laughing. They said the same thing about the Angel of Portugal.

The children said the apparitions of Our Lady left them with a sense of peace and joy, not fun.

At Paris, France in 1830, Our Lady appeared to Catherine Laboure. Catherine described the Virgin as looking very serious with tears in her eyes.

At La Sallete, France in 1846, Our Lady was immersed in tears of sadness when she told the young seers that Rome would lose the faith and become the seat of the antichrist. (Where we are today.)

At Lourdes, France in 1858, Our Lady did not appear smiling or look like she was having fun.

Our Lady of Guadalupe does not appear smiling. Her eyes are downcast, her expression solemn.

In *The Apocalypse* 6:10, Saint John wrote of the martyred saints:

"And they cried with a loud voice, saying: How long, O Lord (Holy and True), dost thou not judge and revenge our blood on them that dwell on the earth?"

They don't sound like they're having fun either.

Nowhere in any apparition or in any earthly contact with Heaven are we presented with evidence that Heaven is a fun place. In fact, all evidence points to the contrary; it points to Heaven being a serious place.

If Heaven isn't fun, then why are we so obsessed with having fun here on earth? Perhaps our pursuit of fun is less about the thrill of fun than about a temporary escape from a meaningless existence. And our lives seem most meaningless when we live them for ourselves and not for God.

Why not focus less on fun and more on going to Heaven? You will have times of intense loneliness, times of sorrow, times of persecution. There's no way around that. But I will be right there with you. I'll walk with you through the valley of tears. I'll be your constant companion through your times of tribulation. Others will be there too. There aren't many of us, but we are here, upholding the last remnants of the Catholic Faith. Won't you join us?

Thank you very much for reading this book. If you enjoyed it, please leave a review so that others will be inspired to read it too. *Your review of this book could actually save someone's soul.* Imagine that.

If you would like clarification about anything you read here, or if I can help you in any way, please contact me.

<u>If you would like to join my Intelligence Report email list and receive expert analysis of world events, email me for details</u>.

You can email me here:

mainsmike@yahoo.com

If you need help in becoming a traditional Catholic, shoot me an email and I'll respond with some information and important websites for you to visit. Don't delay. Your salvation depends on it.

Recommended Reading:

Our Lady of Fatima by William Thomas Walsh

The Truth about What Really Happened to the Catholic Church after Vatican II by Brother Michael Dimond and Brother Peter Dimond

Outside the Catholic Church There is Absolutely No Salvation by Brother Peter Dimond

How to Go to Heaven: Your Proven, Step-by-Step Plan to Achieve Eternal Salvation by Mike Mains

It's all here. Everything you need to go to Heaven, your true home. Read this book and discover for yourself the four key steps that everyone must take if they truly desire to go to Heaven. These four key steps used to be common knowledge among all Catholics, but today *almost nobody is even aware of them.* And yet they contain the one sure way that you can guarantee yourself of going to Heaven. Nothing else you read or do for the rest of your life will ever be more important.

The books *How to Go to Heaven for Teen Boys* and *How to Go to Heaven for Teen Girls* contain the complete text to *How to Go to Heaven*, along with additional chapters on the temptations that young people face, such as drug and alcohol use, immodest dress, the loss of purity, etc.

Other books by Mike Mains

The North Hollywood Detective Club Series

The Case of the Hollywood Art Heist

Teen detectives race to free an innocent man from jail.

The Case of the Dead Man's Treasure

Teen detectives investigating a hit-and-run accident stumble upon the clues to an ancient treasure.

The Case of the Christmas Counterfeiters

Two teen detectives. One criminal mastermind. And two billion dollars in counterfeit currency. What could possibly go wrong?

The Case of the Deadly Double-Cross

Teen detectives are framed for murder.

The Case of the Jilted Juliet

Teen detectives suspect that a girl who committed suicide thirty years ago was actually murdered. Their investigation leads them to a list of suspects that includes their own high school principal.

How to Go to Heaven

Heaven. We all want to go there, but very few of us know how. This book explains the necessary steps one must take to achieve eternal salvation. <u>Nothing else you read or do for the rest of your life will ever be more important.</u>

The books *How to Go to Heaven for Teen Boys* and *How to Go to Heaven for Teen Girls* contain the complete text of *How to Go to Heaven*, along with additional chapters on the temptations young people face.

Monkey Jokes—A Joke Book for Kids!

Tickle your funny bone with these laugh-a-minute jokes for kids. Apes, cheetahs, gorillas, they're all here, ready to entertain you in the world's funniest collection of monkey jokes.

Bodybuilding for Boys & Young Men

If you want muscles and you want them fast, this is the book for you. A fast, fun and effective way to build your body.

Annihilate Your Acne

Do you suffer from acne? Contrary to popular opinion, acne is caused by food allergies and environmental toxins. Eliminate those causes and acne melts away like a snow cone on a hot summer day.